# 500 RECIPES FOR MEALS WITHOUT MEAT

Cheese n potato souffle Page 16.

# 500 RECIPES FOR MEALS WITHOUT MEAT

---

**BY MARGUERITE PATTEN**

**HAMLYN**

LONDON · NEW YORK · SYDNEY · TORONTO

Cover photography by James Jackson

Published by The Hamlyn Publishing Group
Limited
London · New York · Sydney · Toronto
Astronaut House, Feltham, Middlesex, England



First published 1964
Reprinted 1970
Fourth impression 1984

ISBN 0 600 03426 7

Printed in Great Britain by
R. J. Acford

# Contents

*About this book*

● Here are 500 exciting ways to make meals without meat. Whatever you're cooking – a quick snack, a main meal, a picnic lunch or a television supper – you'll find plenty of fascinating recipes from which to choose.

● While not written especially for vegetarians (some recipes using fish are included), they, too, will find this book provides plenty of stimulating ideas for good eating.

● MARGUERITE PATTEN combines the simplest ingredients with imagination and skill to make tasty, light and very nourishing dishes that will appeal to every member of the family.

● Parties are not neglected, either, as a variety of colourful and unusual dips are included. These are quick-to-make and immensely popular with guests of all ages.

● Practical information, such as comparative oven temperatures, useful facts about weights and measures, and hints for obtaining the best results when using these recipes, makes this new cookery book a 'must' for every kitchen.

# Introduction

This book is not written primarily for Vegetarians but it is written to give a very wide selection of recipes that do not include meat, but can be served at main or light meals.
Vegetarians, however, will find many recipes that fit into their diet and, by using vegetarian fat, many others that will be a very pleasant change and give them a well-balanced diet.
Meat is a first-class protein food but, as you will see on page 6, there are other protein foods which are perfectly adequate alternatives and these make the basis for a variety of delicious meals.

# Some Useful Facts and Figures

## Comparison of English and American weights and measures

English weights and measures have been used throughout this book. 3 teaspoons equal 1 tablespoon. The average English teacup is ¼ pint or 1 gill. The average English breakfast cup is ½ pint or 2 gills.
When cups are mentioned in recipes they refer to a B.S.I. measuring cup which holds ½ pint or 10 fluid ounces. The B.S.I. standard tablespoon measures 1 fluid ounce.
In case it is wished to translate any of the weights and measures into their American, Canadian or French counterparts, the following tables give a comparison.

### Liquid Measure

The most important difference to be noted is that the American and Canadian pint is 16 fluid ounces, as opposed to the British Imperial pint, which is 20 fluid ounces. The American ½-pint measuring cup is therefore actually equivalent to two-fifths of a British pint.

### French Weights and Measures

It is difficult to convert to French measures with absolute accuracy, but 1 oz. is equal to approximately 30 grammes, 2 lb. 3 oz. to 1 kilogramme. For liquid measure, approximately 1¾ English pints may be regarded as equal to 1 litre; 1 demilitre is half a litre, and 1 décilitre is one-tenth of a litre.

### Solid Measure

| English | American |
|---|---|
| 1 lb. Butter or other fat | 2 cups |
| 1 lb. Flour | 4 cups |
| 1 lb. Granulated or Castor Sugar | 2 cups |
| 1 lb. Icing or Confectioners' Sugar | 3 cups |
| 1 lb. Brown (moist) Sugar | 2½ cups |
| 1 lb. Golden Syrup or Treacle | 1 cup |
| 1 lb. Rice | 2 cups |
| 1 lb. Dried Fruit | 2 cups |
| 1 lb. Chopped Meat (finely packed) | 2 cups |
| 1 lb. Lentils or Split Peas | 2 cups |
| 1 lb. Coffee (unground) | 2½ cups |
| 1 lb. Soft breadcrumbs | 4 cups |
| ½ oz. Flour | 1 level tablespoon* |
| 1 oz. Flour | 1 heaped tablespoon |
| 1 oz. Sugar | 1 level tablespoon |
| ½ oz. Butter | 1 level tablespoon |
| 1 oz. Golden Syrup or Treacle | 1 level tablespoon |
| 1 oz. Jam or Jelly | 1 level tablespoon |

*must be proper measuring tablespoon

**Oven temperatures**

| | Electricity °F. | Gas Regulo | °C. |
|---|---|---|---|
| COOL oven | 225 to 250 | 0 to ½ | 107 to 121 |
| VERY SLOW oven | 250 to 275 | ½ to 1 | 121 to 135 |
| SLOW oven | 275 to 300 | 1 to 2 | 135 to 149 |
| VERY MODERATE oven | 300 to 350 | 2 to 3 | 149 to 177 |
| MODERATE oven | 375 | 4 | 190 |
| MODERATELY HOT oven | 400 | 5 | 204 |
| HOT oven | 425 to 450 | 6 to 7 | 218 to 233 |
| VERY HOT oven | 475 to 500 | 8 to 9 | 246 to 260 |

**Note**

This table is an approximate guide only.. Different makes of cooker vary and if you are in doubt about the setting it is as well to refer to the manufacturer's temperature chart.

# Kinds of food that take the place of meat

Among the first-class protein foods, of which meat is one, are fish, eggs and cheese. Every one of these, served as a main ingredient, give a really well-balanced meal.
Although of not such great value as the foods above, in that they are generally called a second-class protein, are peas, beans and lentils. They are not a complete substitute for the first-class foods but, on the other hand, they can be used with a very small amount of cheese, etc., to provide an excellent dish.
Vegetarians know the value of nuts and, although most people do not accept them in cooking or savoury dishes, some of the recipes are delicious, as well as nutritious.

## *Value of soups*

A really sustaining soup can be a meal in itself and in this section there are basic recipes using really important foods, i.e. cheese, lentils, etc.
When the recipe does not include milk or cheese you can make it more substantial by putting a good layer of cheese over the top or using partly milk and partly stock.

## *To serve with your soup*

Soup is much more of a meal if it is served with something apart from bread. In this book you will find suggestions for Cheese Shortbread (see page 55) which is excellent with vegetable soups, Melba toast Parmesan (see page 24) is another good accompaniment.
For a crisp topping on soups, cover with **fried croûtons** of bread. Cut the bread into tiny squares and fry in a little hot fat or margarine until crisp and golden brown.
Put on to the soup at the last minute, otherwise they become soft, or they can be served on a separate dish.

# Soups

## Cheese soup No. 1

cooking time 25 minutes

**you will need for 4 servings:**

½ onion (finely chopped)
2 oz. butter or vegetarian fat
1½ oz. flour
1 pint milk
2 teaspoons salt
pinch pepper
1 pint stock
8 oz. grated processed Cheddar cheese
3 carrots (finely chopped or grated)
2 sticks celery or piece of celeriac (finely chopped or grated)

1 Sauté the onion in the butter until tender.
2 Add the flour and cook slowly for a minute, stirring well.
3 Add the milk, seasoning and stock gradually, stirring continuously, and bring to the boil.
4 Add the cheese and stir until melted.
5 Add the carrots and celery and cook until the vegetables are tender, do not boil quickly.
6 Serve hot with caraway seed toast fingers.

## Caraway seed toast fingers

cooking time few minutes

**you will need:**

Slices of bread
butter
caraway seeds

1 Remove the crusts from several slices of bread, cut fairly thin.
2 Butter 1 side and sprinkle with caraway seeds.
3 Toast the buttered side to a golden brown and cut into fingers.

## Cheese soup No. 2

cooking time about 15 minutes

**you will need for 4 servings:**

2 small thinly sliced onions
1½ oz. butter
1½ oz. flour
½ pint white stock or water
1 pint milk
½ level teaspoon salt
pinch cayenne pepper and grated nutmeg
6 oz. small diced Cheddar cheese

1 Cook the onion in the butter for a few minutes without browning.
2 Toss in the flour and stir over a low heat for a further minute.
3 Add the milk and stock or water gradually, and stir until boiling.
4 Season and simmer gently for 5 minutes.
5 Mix in the cheese and reheat without boiling until it has melted.
6 Serve hot with toast or fried croûtons.

## Chestnut soup

cooking time approximately 1 hour

**you will need for 4 servings:**

1 lb. chestnuts
1 pint water or white stock
2 oz. butter
½ pint milk
good pinch salt, cayenne pepper and sugar (if liked)
toast or croûtons

1 Split the skins of the chestnuts, cover with water and cook for 15 minutes.
2 Peel the nuts while still hot, then return to the saucepan with the pint of water or stock.
3 Simmer gently for 45 minutes.
4 Rub the chestnuts through a sieve.
5 Put the purée into the pan, together with the butter, milk and seasoning. Heat slowly, then serve with crisp pieces of toast or croûtons.

## Grape soup

cooking time 20 minutes

**you will need for 4 servings:**

2 lb. grapes (bruised or not quite ripe fruit can be used)
½ pint water
2–3 tablespoons brown sugar
1 teaspoon lemon or orange juice
1 tablespoon cornflour

1 Stew nearly all the grapes until soft with nearly all the water.
2 Rub through a sieve and add brown sugar and lemon or orange juice to the purée.
3 Using rest of cold water mix the cornflour to a smooth paste.
4 Add to the fruit and bring to the boil, stirring to prevent burning.
5 Chill thoroughly and serve with a garnish of fresh grapes.

## Hollandaise soup

cooking time 40–45 minutes

**you will need for 4 servings:**

1 pint milk
piece celery, carrot and onion
2 oz. butter or margarine (1 oz. could be used)
1 oz. flour
2 teaspoons lemon juice
2 eggs
2 tablespoons sherry
seasoning

1 Put the vegetables into the milk, bring gently almost to boiling point, but do not actually boil the milk.
2 Let the vegetables infuse in the milk for about 30 minutes, then strain, and allow the milk to cool.
3 Heat the butter or margarine. Stir in the flour and cook slowly for about 3 minutes, taking care it does not discolour.
4 Take the pan away from the heat and gradually add the cooled milk, stirring well to keep the mixture smooth.
5 Boil steadily until thickened, then reduce heat, add eggs and simmer for about 3–4 minutes.
6 Whisk in the lemon juice, sherry and seasoning, and reheat **without boiling.**

**Variation:**

Follow the recipe as above, adding 2 tablespoons of finely chopped parsley just before serving.

## Lentil soup No. 1

cooking time 12 minutes

**you will need for 4 servings:**

8 oz. lentils
1 large onion
2 carrots
2 tomatoes
1 turnip
2 pints vegetable stock or hot water and yeast extract
salt, paprika
1 teaspoon mixed herbs
1 bay leaf
1 rounded tablespoon butter or margarine
2 tablespoons top milk
chopped fresh chives to garnish

1 Powder lentils in electric grinder.
2 Wash and cut vegetables into small pieces.
3 Put vegetable stock, or hot water and 2 teaspoons yeast extract, into blender.
4 Add vegetables, lentil powder blended with a little of the stock to a smooth paste, herbs, seasoning and fat. Purée in blender, and pour into a large pan.
5 Bring to the boil and simmer for 10 minutes.
6 Lastly add top milk and pour into hot tureen.
7 Garnish with chopped chives.

**Variation:**

### Lentil and parsnip soup

Substitute 2 parsnips for the turnip and follow as in the recipe above.

## Lentil soup No. 2

cooking time $1\frac{3}{4}$ hours

**you will need for 4 servings:**

8 oz. washed lentils
1 onion (chopped)
1 carrot (chopped)
1 pint stock or water
seasoning
little chopped thyme or parsley
1 oz. butter
$\frac{1}{2}$ oz. flour
$\frac{1}{2}$ pint milk
chopped parsley for garnish

1 Put the lentils, onion, carrot and stock into a pan.
2 Add seasoning and thyme and simmer gently for about $1\frac{1}{2}$ hours. The lentils can be soaked overnight if wished.
3 Meanwhile make a very thin sauce with the butter, flour and milk.
4 Add the lentil purée and reheat
5 Season to taste.
6 Garnish with chopped parsley.

**Variations:**

Lentil and celery soup—Use about 6 oz. lentils and 4 oz. chopped celery.

## Tomato and lentil soup

cooking time $1\frac{1}{2}$ hours

**you will need for 4 servings:**

12 oz. tomatoes
2 oz. lentils
$1\frac{1}{2}$ pints stock (preferably bacon stock)
knob butter
salt
pepper
*bouquet garni*

1 Simmer the tomatoes and lentils (which can be soaked overnight in the stock) together with the well-seasoned stock until tender.
2 Either rub through a sieve or, if you skin the tomatoes beforehand, there is no need to sieve, beat the mixture well with a wooden spoon.
3 Heat with the butter, seasoning and herbs for about 5–10 minutes.

## Dried pea soup

cooking time 1¼–1½ hours

**you will need for 4 servings:**

8 oz. dried peas
2 pints stock or water
2 onions
1 carrot
1 turnip
sprig mint
seasoning
1 teaspoon sugar

1 Soak the peas overnight in the stock.
2 Put into saucepan with the vegetables, seasoning and mint and simmer gently for approximately 1¼–1½ hours.
3 Either rub through a sieve or beat until very smooth.
4 Taste and re-season, add sugar.

**Variation:**

Add 2 cloves of garlic to the stock and continue as in the recipe above. Season with plenty of black pepper at the end of cooking.

## Pea soup

When peas are very young it is possible to make this soup with the pea pods only.
Pods from 2 lb. fresh peas can be used instead of the quantity of peas and pods given below.

cooking time 15–20 minutes

**you will need for 4 servings:**

1½ lb. peas (including pods)
1½ pints water or ham stock
small onion (if desired)
salt
pepper
little mint
good pinch sugar
good knob butter

1 Wash pods and shell.
2 Put the pods and peas into the saucepan with stock, the onion, seasoning, little sprig mint and simmer until tender.
3 Rub through a sieve; this must be done very vigorously so only the skins of the pods are left.
4 Return to the pan, reheat, adding a little sugar to taste and butter.
5 Serve garnished with a few freshly cooked peas or chopped mint or some croûtons of fried bread.

**Note:**

If the pods are very fleshy the soup may be a little thick when sieved, so add a small quantity of milk or extra stock.

**Variation:**

Add 1 large finely chopped onion and 2 crushed cloves of garlic to the stock and peas. Continue as with the recipe above.

## White fish soup

cooking time 25 minutes

**you will need for 4 servings:**

12 oz. white fish (plaice, cod, whiting, fresh haddock, etc.)
¾ pint water
small piece onion
seasoning
small sprig parsley, dill, or fennel to flavour
2 oz. butter
1 oz. flour
¾ pint milk
chopped parsley, or chopped dill for garnishing

1 Put the fish, cut into pieces, the water, onion, seasoning and herb or herbs into a saucepan and simmer gently until the fish is only just cooked.
2 Rub through a sieve.
3 Make a sauce of the butter, flour and milk. Add the fish purée, and reheat, adding extra seasoning, if needed.
4 Garnish with chopped parsley, or chopped dill, as desired.

**Variations:**

## Cream of fish soup

Add little cream just before serving, and use slightly less water when cooking the fish.

## Golden fish soup

Use slightly less milk in the sauce. Blend the yolks of 2 eggs with ¼ pint milk or thin cream, add to the fish soup and cook gently, without boiling, for several minutes.

## Fish and potato soup

Cook 2 potatoes with the fish and rub through a sieve. Omit the flour and just add milk and butter and reheat.

# Cooking with Cheese

## *Value*

This is not only an excellent food to serve by itself or with bread, salad, etc., but lends itself to almost infinite variety in cooking.
Cheese dishes need never be dull, and they can be most exciting and attractive to look at, as well as delicious to eat.

## *Cooking*

It is important to select the right type of cheese with which to cook. Cheddar, Cheshire, Lancashire are all good, having a pronounced flavour and good texture.
The Dutch Edam and Gouda and the Danish Samsoe, are also excellent.
If you want a really strong flavour, then grated Parmesan cheese will give it, as it tends to produce a slightly drier mixture. In many recipes the best result is obtained by mixing Parmesan and one of the other cheeses.
The modern processed cheeses are also good for cooking, if you like a more delicate flavour.
Whatever cheese you select for cooking, it is essential not to overcook. If the cheese is going into a sauce, the sauce must be thickened and boiled and the cheese stirred in afterwards.

# Cheese puddings and baked dishes

In this chapter are the popular cheese puddings, and also recipes that are perhaps a little less well-known.
Each and every one of them will provide a main meal in itself.
Serve attractive vegetables with the cheese puddings and, as most of them become fairly firm in texture when cooked, they are delicious if cheese sauce is also served.

### Baked cheese pudding No. 1

cooking time 35 minutes

**you will need for 4 servings:**

½ pint milk
1 oz. butter or margarine
4 oz. breadcrumbs
4 oz. grated Cheddar cheese
1 or 2 eggs
seasoning

1 Bring the milk to the boil.
2 Add the butter or margarine and breadcrumbs.
3 Remove from heat and allow to stand for 5 minutes.
4 Add the cheese and stir in the beaten egg or eggs.
5 Season well and pour the mixture into a well-greased oven-proof dish.
6 Bake in the centre of a hot oven (450°F.—Gas Mark 7) for approximately 30 minutes until brown on top.
7 Serve at once with baked tomatoes.

**Variation:**

Add 1 teaspoon of dried sage with the cheese, and continue as in the recipe above.

### Baked cheese pudding No. 2

cooking time 35 minutes

**you will need for 4 servings:**

¾ pint milk
1½ oz. margarine or butter
3 oz. breadcrumbs
6 oz. grated cheese
seasoning
2 eggs

1 Bring the milk to the boil, add the margarine or butter and breadcrumbs.
2 Take off heat and stand on one side for 5 minutes.
3 Add the cheese and season well.
4 Stir in the beaten eggs.
5 Half fill with the mixture a well-greased fireproof dish and bake in the centre of a hot oven (450°F.—Gas Mark 7) for approximately 35 minutes, until brown on top. Serve at once with baked tomatoes.

This is a rather less substantial recipe than Baked Cheese Pudding No. 1 as proportions of bread are less.

## Tomato cheese pudding

cooking time 35 minutes + 30 minutes to stand

**you will need for 4 servings:**

¾ pint milk
2 eggs
4 oz. breadcrumbs
4 oz. grated cheese
pinch salt and pepper
pinch dry mustard
2–3 large tomatoes

1 Warm the milk to blood heat, whisk on to the beaten eggs.
2 Add the breadcrumbs.
3 Allow to stand for 30 minutes.
4 Stir in the cheese and seasoning.
5 Line a greased dish with the sliced tomatoes and pour in cheese mixture.
6 Bake in a moderate oven (375°F.—Gas Mark 4) for 30 minutes until brown and just set.
7 Serve at once.

**Variations on cheese pudding:**

Whichever of the cheese pudding recipes you choose, the following variations can be made:

## Asparagus cheese pudding

Either add the contents of a small can of asparagus tips or a little cooked asparagus to the ingredients, or use rather thin asparagus soup in place of milk in either recipe.

## Mushroom cheese pudding

Either add 2–3 oz. chopped fried mushrooms to the milk, or fairly thin mushroom soup in place of milk.

## Savoury cheese pudding

Add about 1 tablespoon of freshly chopped parsley and 1 teaspoon chopped capers, 1 teaspoon of chopped gherkins to the cheese, etc.

## Bread and cheese bake

cooking time approximately 50 minutes

**you will need for 4 servings:**

little butter
1 level teaspoon oregano (or other herb)
8 thin slices day-old bread, buttered
8 slices Cheddar cheese (about same size as bread slices)
3 eggs
1 teaspoon made mustard
1 level teaspoon salt
good grinding pepper
1 tablespoon chopped onion
1½ pints milk
paprika

1 Butter a large shallow oven dish (about 12 x 7 x 2 inches).
2 Dust oregano lightly over the bottom.
3 Arrange 4 slices bread on bottom (cutting to fit).
4 Cover with double slices of cheese and top with remaining bread.
5 Beat eggs well; add seasonings and onion and then milk, mixing well.
6 Pour this over the bread and sprinkle with paprika.
7 Stand in a pan with 1-inch hot water and bake in a moderate oven (375°F.—Gas Mark 4) for about 50 minutes until lightly set and golden.
8 Serve at once, with hot green vegetables or salad.

## Cheese Charlotte

cooking time about 45 minutes

**you will need for 4 servings:**

2–3 eggs
1 teaspoon mustard
seasoning
1 pint milk
4–5 slices bread and butter
4–6 oz. grated cheese

1 Beat the eggs, add mustard, seasoning and milk.
2 Put a layer of bread and butter in a dish, and most of the cheese. Cover with the rest of the bread and butter and cheese.
3 Pour over the savoury custard mixture.
4 Bake in the centre of a moderate oven (375°F.—Gas Mark 4) until golden brown and puffy—about 45 minutes.
5 Serve hot with salad or green vegetables.

**Variations:**

## Cheese and asparagus Charlotte

Use ½ pint asparagus soup, ½ pint milk instead of all milk.

## Cheese and mushroom Charlotte

Use ½ pint mushroom soup, ½ pint milk instead of all milk.

## Cheese and tomato Charlotte

Use 1 pint tomato juice instead of milk.

## Celery cheese pie

cooking time 35 minutes

**you will need for 4 servings:**

1 head celery
1 oz. margarine
1 oz. flour
¼ pint milk
6 oz. grated cheese
seasoning
2 tablespoons tomato ketchup or purée
1 egg
1 lb. mashed potato
2 tomatoes

1 Chop and cook celery in salted water.
2 Lay in bottom of pie dish—saving ¼ pint stock.
3 Make a white sauce with the margarine, flour, milk and celery stock.
4 Season well, stir in most of the cheese and tomato purée and lastly the beaten egg—do not boil.
5 Pour sauce over celery.
6 Top with mashed potato, rest of cheese and sliced tomatoes.
7 Cook for approximately 20–25 minutes towards the top of a moderately hot oven (375°F.—Gas Mark 4).

**Variation:**

## Leek cheese pie

Substitute leeks for celery and continue as in the recipe above.

## Cheese and potato shape

cooking time 30 minutes

**you will need for 4 servings:**

2 oz. vegetarian margarine
4 oz. cooked new potatoes
2 large tomatoes
6 oz. sliced Cheddar cheese
½ pint cheese sauce (see page 63)

1 Brush sides of mould with margarine.
2 Put in a layer of sliced potatoes, skinned and sliced tomatoes and cheese.
3 Fill dish in this manner, and cover top with remainder of melted margarine.
4 Bake for 30 minutes in a moderately hot oven (375°F.—Gas Mark 4).
5 Turn out and coat with cheese sauce.

**Variation:**

Follow the recipe as above but add 2 sliced courgettes. Stir-fry for a few minutes and layer with potatoes, tomatoes and Cheddar cheese.

## Cheese and carrot shape

Recipe as Cheese and potato shape (see above) but use 8 oz. cooked sliced young carrots.

## Cheese and mushroom batter

cooking time 30 minutes

**you will need for 4 servings:**

½ pint pouring batter (page 66)
4 oz. grated cheese
1 oz. butter
8 medium-sized mushrooms
seasoning

1 Add cheese to batter.
2 Put mushrooms into an ovenproof dish, a dab of butter on each and season well.
3 Bake at 400°F.—Gas Mark 5 for 5 minutes.
4 Pour in the batter and return to oven at 425°F.—Gas Mark 6 for about 25 minutes.

## Cheese and onion roll

cooking time 30–35 minutes

**you will need for 4 servings:**

1 large onion
2 oz. butter
2 oz. white breadcrumbs
4 oz. grated Cheddar cheese
1 level teaspoon chopped parsley
salt and pepper
4 oz. flaky or puff pastry (see page 54)
1 egg

1 Cook the finely sliced onion in butter until transparent.
2 Stir in the breadcrumbs, toss in pan until crisp and remove from heat.
3 Add the cheese, parsley and seasoning to taste.
4 Roll out pastry to an oblong about 10 x 6 inches, brush edges with beaten egg.
5 Spread the filling over the pastry, roll up short sides and seal the edges.
6 Brush over with egg and bake at 450°F.—Gas Mark 7 for 15 minutes.
7 Reduce heat to 375°F.—Gas Mark 7 for 15 minutes.
8 Serve hot or cold.

## Cheese and mushroom roll

Recipe as cheese and onion roll (see above), but substitute 4 oz. cooked mushrooms for the fried onion.
These can be left whole if small, or chopped if large.

## Cheese fluff

cooking time 25–30 minutes

**you will need for 4 servings:**

3 eggs
½ pint milk
4 oz. grated cheese
2 teaspoons parsley
good pinch pepper
¼ level teaspoon mustard
good pinch salt
2 oz. breadcrumbs

1 Blend the egg yolks with the warm milk, cheese and parsley.
2 Add seasoning and pour mixture over the breadcrumbs and leave until cold.
3 Whisk the egg whites with a pinch of salt until stiff.
4 Fold into the breadcrumb mixture and pour into greased soufflé dish.
5 Bake for 30 minutes in centre of moderately hot oven (375°F.—Gas Mark 5) for 25–30 minutes.

**Variations:**

## Curried cheese fluff

Blend 1 level teaspoon curry powder with the egg yolks.

## Herb cheese fluff

Add 1 teaspoon chopped fresh parsley, ½ teaspoon chopped fresh sage, ½ teaspoon grated lemon rind, to egg yolk.

## Cheddar cheese and gherkin loaves

cooking time 35–40 minutes

**you will need for 4 servings:**

4 gherkins
4 oz. Cheddar cheese
8 oz. self-raising flour (with plain flour 2 level teaspoons baking powder)
½ teaspoon salt
¼ teaspoon dry mustard
pinch cayenne pepper
2 oz. butter
1 beaten egg
¼ pint milk

1 Chop gherkins and grate cheese.
2 Sift flour and seasonings together.
3 Rub in butter, add cheese and gherkins and mix into a soft dough with egg and milk.
4 Transfer to 2 greased loaf tins* and bake in centre of a moderately hot oven (400°F.—Gas Mark 5) for 35–40 minutes.
5 Allow to cool in tins for 10 minutes, then remove from tins and place on wire tray.

*Instead of the loaf tins, two 1 lb. cocoa or baking powder tins may be used, when baking time will be about 40–45 minutes.

## Cheese pie de luxe

cooking time 25–30 minutes

**you will need for 4 servings:**

8 oz. cheese pastry (see page 53)

**For filling:**

1 medium onion
8 oz. cooked and diced potato
2 oz. cooked peas
4 oz. cooked and diced carrots
salt and pepper to taste
½ level teaspoon mixed herbs
little milk or egg to glaze

1 Make pastry and divide in half.
2 Roll out one half and line an 8-inch well-greased oven-proof plate.
3 Moisten edges of pastry with water.
4 Chop onion coarsely and mix all filling ingredients together.
5 Pile into the centre of the pastry case and cover with remaining pastry rolled out slightly larger than the plate.
6 Press edges well together to seal, then knock up with the back of a knife.
7 Brush top with a little milk or beaten egg and decorate with pastry leaves, rolled and cut from trimmings.
8 Bake in the centre of a hot oven (425°–450°F.—Gas Mark 6–7) for 25–30 minutes.
9 Serve hot or cold with salad.

## Cheese, potato and onion pie

cooking time 30 minutes

**you will need for 4 servings:**

8 oz. short crust pastry (see page 55)

**For filling:**

8 oz. diced cooked potatoes
4 oz. grated cheese
1 small grated onion
salt and pepper
pinch mixed herbs
little milk if required

1 Roll out half of the pastry to ⅛ inch thickness and line a 7-inch greased sandwich tin.
2 Mix all ingredients well together, moistening with a little milk if necessary.
3 Spread in lined tin and cover with second half of pastry; decorate with leaves of pastry.
4 Bake in hot oven in the centre (450°F.—Gas Mark 7) for 30 minutes.

## Cheese, potato and mushroom pie

Use 2–4 oz. chopped mushrooms instead of the grated onion in cheese, potato and onion pie (see page 13).

## Cheese popovers

cooking time 20–25 minutes

**you will need for 4 servings:**

butter
4 oz. flour
$\frac{1}{4}$ teaspoon salt
2 eggs
scant $\frac{1}{2}$ pint milk
2 oz. grated Cheddar cheese
pinch cayenne

1 Put a knob of butter in the centre of each little tin of a bun tray and place in a hot oven (450°F.—Gas Mark 7) for about 5–7 minutes until the butter is thoroughly hot.
2 To make the batter, sieve the flour and salt into a mixing basin. Beat the eggs well and add the milk to them. Stir the liquid ingredients into the sieved ingredients and beat well until thoroughly blended.
3 Pour a scant tablespoon of the batter into each tin. Put a teaspoon of grated Cheddar cheese in the centre of each and cover with a teaspoon of batter.
4 Bake in a very hot oven (475°F.—Gas Mark 8) for approximately 15 minutes until well risen, crisp and golden brown.

## Cheese, potato and tomato mould

cooking time approximately 40 minutes

**you will need for 4 servings:**

$\frac{1}{3}$ pint cheese sauce (see page 63)
seasoning
1 lb. potatoes
8 oz. tomatoes
crisp breadcrumbs

1 Make the sauce and season well.
2 Cook the potatoes until just tender.
3 Allow to cool and cut into slices about $\frac{1}{3}$ inch thick—keeping the slices whole.
4 Skin and slice the tomatoes.
5 Grease a medium-sized cake tin or pie dish and line the bottom and sides with breadcrumbs.
6 Put a layer of potato at the bottom, then a layer of tomato and cover with cheese sauce.
7 Repeat layers until all the ingredients are used up, ending with a layer of potato.
8 Cover with a piece of greased paper and bake in the centre of a moderate oven (375°F.—Gas Mark 4) for 40 minutes.
9 Turn out and serve hot.

### Variation:

Follow the recipe as above, but add fried thinly sliced onion rings on top of the tomato layers.

# Cheese soufflés and mousses

The soufflé is probably one of the best known ways of using cheese, and even when a basic recipe is followed (see below) it can be varied a great deal by the choice of the cheese. Parmesan cheese gives a very fine texture and rather dry result.
The soft type of processed cheese gives a more creamy and less definite flavour.
The important things to remember are that you must cook the sauce well, beat in the egg yolks and cheese when it is no longer boiling, and fold in the stiffly beaten egg whites carefully. The cooking times given produce a soufflé that is just set, but if you like a softer one, take it out 5 minutes earlier.
Always time a soufflé so that it finishes cooking when the family is ready to eat it.

### To prepare a soufflé dish

For a hot soufflé, butter well and allow plenty of space for the soufflé to rise.
If you feel it is going to be badly supported as it rises, because the dish is small, tie a band of buttered paper around, so it comes above the top of the soufflé dish.

## Cheese soufflé

cooking time 30–35 minutes

**you will need for 4 servings:**

4 eggs or 3 yolks and 4 whites
1 oz. vegetarian fat, butter or margarine
$\frac{1}{4}$ pint milk
$\frac{1}{2}$ oz. wholemeal flour or up to 1 oz. ordinary flour
seasoning
*3–5 oz. grated cheese

1 Separate the eggs.
2 Heat the fat, stir in flour, cook for several minutes and add the milk gradually.
3 Bring to the boil and cook until thickened, then add the seasoning, cheese and beaten egg yolks.
4 Finally fold in the stiffly beaten egg whites.
5 Put into a prepared soufflé dish, and bake in the centre of a moderately hot oven (400°F.—Gas Mark 5) until well risen and golden brown, i.e. approximately 30–35 minutes. Serve at once.

*A mixture of Cheddar and Parmesan gives an excellent flavour, or use a soft cream cheese, with a very little Parmesan.

**Variations:**

## Cheese and carrot

Use ½ pint thick carrot purée instead of milk.

## Cheese and spinach

Use ½ pint thick spinach purée instead of milk—cook a little longer at 375°F.—Gas Mark 4.

## Cheese and tomato

Use ⅜ pint tomato purée—made by rubbing tomatoes through a sieve—or ¼ pint tomato juice instead of milk.

## Cheese and mushroom soufflé

Ingredients as Cheese soufflé (see above) except 2 oz. finely chopped cooked mushrooms can be added, or use ⅓-pint concentrated mushroom soup in place of milk.

## Cheese and cauliflower soufflé

cooking time 45 minutes

**you will need for 4 servings:**

1 small cauliflower
1 oz. butter
1 oz. flour
¼ pint milk
seasoning
3 eggs
4 oz. grated Cheddar cheese

1 Cook and drain cauliflower.
2 Melt butter in a saucepan and add flour, stirring constantly, cook for 1–2 minutes.
3 Add milk gradually, stirring well and cook for a further minute.
4 Season well and allow to cool.
5 Separate eggs and beat yolks and cheese into mixture.
6 Separate cauliflower into very small sprigs and cover bottom of soufflé dish, using about half the cauliflower.
7 Whisk egg whites until thick enough to form peaks; fold into the cheese mixture.
8 Pour half the mixture over the cauliflower.
9 Repeat the layers, ending with soufflé mixture.
10 Bake in the centre of a moderately hot oven (400°F.—Gas Mark 5) for approximately 30–35 minutes until golden brown.
11 Serve at once.

## Cheese and chestnut soufflé

Use the same recipe as Cheese and cauliflower soufflé (see above), cooking the chestnuts and peeling, and then arranging in layers in place of the cauliflower sprigs.
Or cook the chestnuts and make a purée, then follow exactly the Cheese and potato soufflé (see page 16) with purée of chestnuts instead of potatoes.

## Cheese and haddock soufflé

cooking time 25 minutes

**you will need for 4 servings:**

4–5 oz. smoked haddock
1 oz. butter
½ oz. flour
scant ¼ pint milk
seasoning
1 oz. Parmesan cheese (grated)
1 or 2 tablespoons cream
3 egg yolks
4 egg whites

1 The haddock may be used cooked or raw as preferred. If using raw fish, remove skin and pound the fish until smooth; if cooked, flake finely.
2 Make a thick sauce of the butter, flour and milk.
3 Add the haddock and seasoning. Do not add much salt to the mixture, since the smoked haddock gives a salt taste.
4 Add the cheese, cream and beaten egg yolks; mix well.
5 Fold in the stiffly beaten egg whites, then pour into prepared soufflé dish and bake in the centre of a moderately hot oven (400°F.—Gas Mark 5) for approximately 25 minutes, until golden brown and well risen.
Serve at once.

## Cheese soufflé tarts

cooking time 12–15 minutes

**you will need for 4 servings:**

4 oz. short crust pastry (see page 55)
2 eggs
2 oz. finely grated cheese
pinch cayenne
good pinch salt, pinch pepper
½ teaspoon chopped parsley
watercress for garnish

1. Roll out the pastry very thinly and line 9 or 12 patty tins with this.
2. Beat the egg yolks with the cheese and seasonings, add the parsley, and lastly the stiffly beaten egg whites.
3. Put into the pastry cases and bake for approximately 12–15 minutes in centre of a hot oven (450°F.—Gas Mark 7).
4. Serve hot or cold garnished with watercress.

## Cheese and potato soufflé

cooking time 40–45 minutes

**you will need for 4 servings:**

1 lb. potatoes
⅛ pint hot milk
2 oz. butter or margarine
4 eggs
3 oz. grated Cheddar cheese
1 tablespoon finely chopped parsley
1 teaspoon salt

1. Cook and mash the potatoes.
2. Add the milk, butter, or margarine, cheese, parsley and salt.
3. Separate eggs; stir in the beaten yolks and fold in the stiffly beaten whites to the mixture.
4. Pour into a soufflé dish and bake for approximately 25–30 minutes in the centre of a moderately hot oven (400°F.—Gas Mark 5).
5. Serve at once.

## Cheese and vegetable soufflé

cooking time approximately 35 minutes

**you will need for 4 servings:**

12 oz. cooked mixed vegetables (diced)
½ pint milk or vegetable stock
1 oz. semolina
2 eggs
salt and pepper
1 teaspoon mixed mustard
4 oz. grated cheese
1 level teaspoon baking powder

1. Grease a casserole or soufflé dish.
2. Put vegetables in the bottom of the dish.
3. Warm the milk, sprinkle in semolina, bring to boil stirring all the time, and boil for 7 minutes, making sure the semolina is cooked.
4. Cool slightly, add beaten eggs and seasoning.
5. Lastly add cheese and baking powder, saving 1 oz. of the cheese for topping, mixing thoroughly.
6. Place the mixture on top of the vegetables in the casserole and sprinkle with remaining cheese.
7. Cook in centre of moderately hot oven (400°F.—Gas Mark 5) for 20–25 minutes. Serve immediately.

## Rich cheese soufflé

cooking time 1 hour

**you will need for 4 servings:**

½ pint thick white sauce (see page 63)
4 eggs
3 oz. cooked rice
4 oz. grated cheese
1–2 tablespoons chopped parsley
¼ teaspoon nutmeg
¼ teaspoon paprika
½ teaspoon basil or powdered sage

1. Make white sauce.
2. Separate eggs and beat yolks into sauce gradually.
3. Blend in rice, cheese, parsley and seasonings.
4. Beat egg whites until stiff but not dry. Fold into the rice mixture.
5. Pour into a greased 2-pint casserole or soufflé dish and bake in centre of very moderate oven (350°F.—Gas Mark 3) for 45 minutes.

**Variations:**

### Onion and rice soufflé

Substitute 1 or 2 boiled and chopped onions for the cheese.

### Tomato and rice soufflé

Use tomato sauce or concentrated tomato soup instead of white sauce.

## Cheese and tomato puff

cooking time 35–40 minutes

**you will need for 4 servings:**

1½ oz. margarine
1 small finely chopped onion
3 skinned tomatoes
½ pint water
2 oz. semolina
seasoning
4 oz. grated cheese
2 large or 3 standard eggs

1. Heat margarine and fry onion and tomatoes until a smooth mixture.
2. Add the water and bring to the boil.
3. Shake in the semolina and stir until well blended.

4 Cook for a good 5 minutes, stirring most of the time, until thickened.
5 Add seasoning, cheese and beaten eggs.
6 Put in soufflé or pie dish and bake for approximately 25–30 minutes in the centre of a moderately hot oven (400°F.—Gas Mark 5) until firm and golden brown.

**Variation:**

Follow the recipe as above but add 1 teaspoon dried parsley with the seasoning, cheese and beaten eggs.

## Blue cheese mousse

cooking time few minutes

**you will need for 4 servings:**

4 oz. blue cheese
⅛ pint thin cream
¼ pint thick cream
rounds of brown bread

1 Press the cheese through a fine sieve.
2 Add thin cream and mix thoroughly.
3 Place in top of a double saucepan over boiling water and stir until smooth.
4 Remove from heat and chill.
5 Beat in thick cream.
6 Turn the mixture into a shallow mould and freeze for 4 hours, or until the mousse is firm.
7 Unmould on to a chilled serving dish and decorate with rounds of brown bread.

**Variation:**

This mousse also makes an excellent dip. Pour it into small bowls, sprinkle with paprika and serve with cauliflower florets, carrot strips or small biscuits.

## Cheese mousse

cooking time 10 minutes

**you will need for 4 servings:**

1 oz. butter
1 oz. flour
½ pint milk
2 oz. finely grated Cheddar cheese
1 oz. Parmesan cheese
2 eggs
1 heaped teaspoon tomato purée
1 heaped teaspoon French mustard
pinch salt and cayenne
1 heaped teaspoon powdered gelatine

1 Prepare a 5-inch soufflé dish by tying a wide band of double greaseproof paper round the outside so that it extends above the rim.
2 Melt the butter, stir in the flour and cook for 1 minute.
3 Add the milk gradually, bring to the boil and boil for 1 minute, stirring.
4 Add the cheese, purée and seasoning, stir until smooth.
5 Soften the gelatine in 1 tablespoon of cold water and dissolve in 2 tablespoons of boiling water.
6 Separate eggs; add the beaten yolks and dissolved gelatine to the cheese sauce, stirring over the gentle heat until it thickens.
7 Cool, stirring occasionally and, when almost set, fold in the stiffly beaten whites.
8 Pour into the soufflé dish and put in a cool place to set.
9 Remove the paper carefully, and serve with a lettuce salad.

**Variations:**

### Cream cheese mousse

Recipe as Cheese mousse, but substitute 3–4 oz. soft cream cheese for other cheeses.

### Camembert mousse

Recipe as Cheese mousse, but use 2–3 oz. Camembert cheese, removing rind before weighing.

### Tomato cheese mousse

Recipe as Cheese mousse, but in place of ½ pint of milk, use ½ pint of either tomato juice or strained tomato purée.

# Fried cheese dishes

Cheese is delicious, whether fried in slices or as part of fritters, etc.
It is, however, essential that you do not overcook the cheese, for then, not only does the dish become spoilt as the cheese gets oily and tough, but it also tends to lose its shape.
Cheese fritters and other recipes in this section cannot be called a meal in themselves, but served with a crisp salad, which makes a very good contrast to the richness of the dish, they are very tasty. On the other hand, tomatoes, mushrooms, or a green vegetable, are all suitable accompaniments.

## Cheese aigrettes

cooking time about 15 minutes

**you will need for 2 servings:**

1 oz. butter or margarine
¼ pint water
2 oz. flour
1½ oz. finely grated Cheddar cheese
good pinch salt
cayenne
2 well-beaten egg yolks
fat for deep frying
little grated cheese
parsley or watercress for garnish

1 Add the margarine or butter to the water and bring to the boil.
2 Heat until the fat is melted.
3 Stir in the flour and continue heating, stirring all the time, until the mixture leaves the sides of the pan.
4 Take off the heat, add the grated cheese, seasoning and lastly the yolks.
5 Allow the mixture to get quite cold.
6 Heat as much fat or oil as your pan holds, until a faint haze is seen.
7 Drop small spoonfuls of the mixture into the deep hot fat, immediately turning the heat as low as possible. This allows the aigrettes to cook through to the middle without becoming too brown on the outside.
8 When crisp and brown, drain carefully and pile on to a hot dish, sprinkling with seasoning and a little more grated cheese.
9 Garnish with parsley or watercress.

## Cheese cutlets

cooking time about 15 minutes

**you will need for 4 servings:**

1 oz. margarine
1 oz. flour
¼ pint milk
seasoning
2 oz. fine breadcrumbs
3 oz. grated cheese
**For coating:**
1 egg
crisp breadcrumbs
**For frying:**
fat

1 Make a thick sauce of the margarine, flour and milk.
2 Season very well.
3 Add breadcrumbs and cheese.
4 Form into cutlet shapes when cold.
5 Coat with beaten egg and breadcrumbs and fry in smoking fat until crisp golden brown.

**Variations:**

### Cheese rice cutlets

Recipe as above but use 2 oz. cooked rice instead of breadcrumbs.

### Cheese and vegetable cutlets

Recipe as above but substitute approximately 6 oz. cooked chopped vegetables for breadcrumbs.

## Cheese fritters No. 1

cooking time 8–10 minutes

**you will need for 2 servings:**

2 eggs
2 oz. grated cheese
2 oz. flour
seasoning
little fat for frying

1 Blend the ingredients together.
2 Drop spoonfuls into hot fat in the frying pan
3 Fry on either side until golden brown.

## Cheese fritters No. 2

cooking time about 5 minutes

**you will need for 4 servings:**

4 oz. self-raising flour (with plain flour use 1 teaspoon baking powder)
good pinch salt, pepper, mustard
1 beaten egg
just under ⅓ pint milk
3 oz. finely grated cheese
fat or oil for frying (deep or shallow)

1 Sieve the flour with the seasonings.
2 Beat in the egg, milk and cheese.
3 Drop spoonfuls of mixture into hot fat. Fry until crisp and golden brown, turning over if using shallow fat.

**Variations:**

### Cheese and asparagus fritters

Use asparagus soup instead of milk.

### Cheese and celery fritters

Add 2 tablespoons chopped cooked celery and use celery stock in place of milk.

### Cheese and corn fritters

Add 3 oz. cooked corn.

### Cheese and mushroom fritters

Either use mushroom soup instead of milk, or add 2 oz. very finely chopped cooked mushrooms to the flour, mixture and reducing the cheese to 2 oz.

## Cheese and tomato fritters

Use tomato juice or purée in place of milk.

## Potato cheese fritters

cooking time about 8 minutes

**you will need for 4 servings:**

2 rounded tablespoons self-raising flour (with plain flour use 1 level teaspoon baking powder)
1¼ lb. raw potatoes
8 oz. grated cheese
½ level teaspoon salt
fat for frying

1 Peel the potatoes and grate finely.
2 Mix in the flour, cheese and salt.
3 Put tablespoon of the mixture into a frying pan containing fat at frying temperature, about ½ inch deep.
4 Fry gently, browning on both sides.
5 Lift from the fat and drain on kitchen paper.
6 Serve hot.

## Cheese meringues

cooking time 5 minutes

**you will need for 4 servings:**

2 egg whites
2 oz. finely grated Parmesan cheese
seasoning
deep fat or oil for frying

1 Whisk the egg whites until very stiff.
2 Mix the cheese and seasoning, fold into the egg whites gently and carefully.
3 Drop spoonfuls into the very hot fat. To test for the right heat, the fat should brown a small cube of bread within ½ minute.
4 Fry for 1–2 minutes, until crisp and golden brown; then bring out, drain and serve them piping hot.

## Cheese and rice balls No. 1

cooking time 25–30 minutes

**you will need for 2 servings:**

1 pint water
½ teaspoon salt
1 small very finely chopped onion
3 oz. rice
3 oz. grated cheese
2 teaspoons chopped parsley
pinch mixed herbs
good pinch pepper and mustard
oil or fat for frying

**To coat:**

1 egg
breadcrumbs

1 Bring the water to the boil, add the salt, and onion, then stir in the rice.
2 Continue cooking, stirring well from time to time until the mixture is very thick, approximately 20 minutes.
3 Add the cheese, parsley and herbs; season well.
4 Let the mixture cook, then form into balls.
5 Dip into the beaten egg and coat with breadcrumbs.
6 Fry in smoking fat until crisp and brown.

**Variations:**

### Mushroom rice balls

Fry about 3 oz. finely chopped mushrooms in pan before adding water, rice, etc. and omit cheese.

### Prawn rice balls

Omit cheese, substitute 3–4 oz. finely chopped prawns or shrimps. Serve with anchovy sauce.

### Tomato rice balls

Use ½ pint tomato juice and ½ pint water instead of 1 pint water.

## Cheese and rice balls No. 2

cooking time 25 minutes

**you will need for 4 servings:**

3 oz. round or medium grain rice
1 level teaspoon salt

**For the sauce:**

3 level dessertspoons cornflour
1 tablespoon oil
½ pint milk
3 oz. Parmesan cheese
½ level teaspoon dry mustard
dash cayenne
salt
1 level teaspoon paprika
1 teaspoon grated onion
few drops Worcestershire sauce

**For coating:**

1 beaten egg
crisp breadcrumbs
oil or fat for frying

1 Cook rice in boiling salted water for approximately 15 minutes until tender. Drain thoroughly.
2 Make sauce with the oil, cornflour and milk, add rice and all other ingredients. Mix well and set aside to chill.
3 Divide into about 8 good solid balls and coat with egg and breadcrumbs.
4 Fry in oil or fat heated to 375°F.—Gas Mark 4 for approximately 2–3 minutes until a cube of bread turns golden brown in ½ minute.
5 Drain and serve hot or cold, with hot green vegetables or salad.

**Note:**

If fried too long the balls will break.

## Crusty cheese balls

cooking time 5 minutes

**you will need for 4 servings:**

- 1 lb. grated sharp cheese
- 3 oz. flour
- 8 drops Tabasco sauce
- 1 teaspoon Worcestershire sauce
- 1 tablespoon chopped parsley
- 1 teaspoon salt
- 1 teaspoon paprika
- 2 stiffly beaten egg whites

1 Combine cheese and flour.
2 Stir in Tabasco, Worcestershire sauce, parsley and seasonings.
3 Mix in egg whites.
4 Roll mixture into balls about the size of a walnut and either deep fry in hot oil, or shallow fry in ½-inch oil until a light brown.
5 Drain on kitchen paper and serve warm.

**Variation:**

Follow the recipe as above, adding 1 teaspoon dried sage instead of the parsley and paprika.

## Cheesy tomatoes

cooking time 2–3 minutes

**you will need for 2–3 servings:**

- 8 small firm tomatoes
- 2 oz. grated cheese
- salt
- cayenne
- little seasoned flour
- 1 beaten egg
- brown breadcrumbs
- fat for frying

1 Skin and core the tomatoes.
2 Stuff tightly with the cheese seasoned well with salt and cayenne.
3 Roll in flour.
4 Dip in egg and coat well with breadcrumbs.
5 Fry in hot fat until a golden brown.
6 Serve cold with salad.

**Variation:**

Sprinkle a pinch of mixed fresh or dried herbs into each tomato and follow the recipe as above.

# Cheese and vegetable dishes

Cheese blends extremely well with the majority of vegetables, whether cooked vegetables are served with a cheese sauce, or the cheese is mixed with the vegetables.

## Cheese beans

cooking time 40 minutes

**you will need for 4 servings:**

- 1 lb. sliced green beans
- 1 small grated onion
- seasoning
- ½ pint white sauce (see page 63)
- 2 oz. grated cheese
- 2 tablespoons breadcrumbs
- knobs butter

1 Cook the beans with the onion and seasoning.
2 Strain and put half the bean and onion mixture into a baking dish.
3 Cover with half the sauce and half the cheese.
4 Add the remaining beans and cheese and top with breadcrumbs and knobs of butter.
5 Bake in a moderate oven (375°F.—Gas Mark 4) for 20 minutes until crisp and brown.

## Cheese and vegetable pie No. 1

cooking time 30–40 minutes

**you will need for 4 servings:**

- 2–3 skinned, sliced tomatoes
- 1 lb. cooked chopped vegetables
- medium can baked beans
- ½ pint white sauce
- salt and pepper
- 1 tablespoon chopped parsley
- 4 oz. grated cheese
- 6 oz. short crust pastry (page 55)
- beaten egg or milk for glazing

1 Fill a pie dish with tomatoes and all vegetables.
2 Add white sauce.
3 Stir in a good pinch of salt and pepper, chopped parsley and cheese.
4 Roll the pastry into a round to fit the top of the pie dish, damp the edges of the dish and cover with pastry.
5 Flute the edges of the pastry lid and make a hole in the centre of the pie.
6 Cut a few leaves from the remaining scraps of pastry, brush with beaten egg or milk and press into position on the pie. Glaze the pastry lid with egg or milk.

7 Bake in a hot oven (425°F.—Gas Mark 6) for 10 minutes. Reduce heat to moderate (375°F. —Gas Mark 4) and cook for a further 20–30 minutes until the pastry is golden brown.

## Cheese and vegetable pie No. 2

cooking time 35 minutes

**you will need for 4 servings:**

- 1 large packet mixed frozen vegetables
- 1 lb. mashed potatoes
- 3 oz. grated cheese
- little butter
- ½ pint cheese sauce (see page 63)

1 Cook the frozen vegetables as directed on the packet.
2 Beat a good knob of butter and half the cheese with the mashed potato until very soft and creamy.
3 Drain cooked vegetables, mix with the cheese sauce and put into a pie dish.
4 Top with the potatoes and cook for 20 minutes in a moderately hot oven (400°F.—Gas Mark 5).
5 The remaining cheese can either be sprinkled on just before serving or put over the potatoes before baking.

## Stuffed vegetable marrow

cooking time 20 minutes

**you will need for 4 servings:**

- 1 medium sized marrow
- 1 large packet frozen peas and carrots
- 2 oz. grated cheese
- ½ pint cheese sauce (see page 63)
- few breadcrumbs
- seasoning

1 Peel marrow and cut into fairly thick rings, season and put in a steamer over a pan of boiling water.
2 Cook for approximately 12 minutes, or until tender, but not watery.
3 Meanwhile peas and carrots should also be cooked according to directions on the packet, and the sauce made.
4 Lift the rings of marrow on to a heatproof dish, draining well.
5 Blend the cooked and drained peas and carrots with the cheese sauce, and put in the centre of each marrow ring.
6 Top with grated cheese and breadcrumbs and brown for a few minutes under the grill.

**Variations:**

Use tomato sauce—see page 65—instead of cheese sauce.
Use barbecue sauce—see page 62—instead of cheese sauce.

## Onion and cheese pie

cooking time 30 minutes

**you will need for 4 servings:**

- 8 oz. short crust pastry (see page 55)
- 4 large cooked onions
- 2 eggs
- 2 oz. grated Cheddar cheese
- seasoning
- egg or milk to glaze

1 Line a pie plate with half the pastry.
2 Drain the onions well and cut into neat pieces.
3 Arrange onions on pastry.
4 Beat the eggs and add the cheese and seasoning.
5 Pour over the onions and cover with the remaining pastry, sealing the edges.
6 Brush the top with a little egg or milk and bake in the centre of a hot oven (450°F.—Gas Mark 7) for 20 minutes.
7 Reduce to moderate oven (375°F.—Gas Mark 4) for a further 10 minutes.
8 Serve hot or cold.

## Parmesan potato pie

cooking time about 45 minutes

**you will need for 4 servings:**

- 2 lb. potatoes
- ½ pint milk
- 1 beaten egg
- 4 oz. grated Parmesan cheese
- salt and pepper
- 1 oz. butter

1 Cook potatoes.
2 Mash them and add the milk, beating very thoroughly.
3 Add egg, cheese and seasoning.
4 Pile into a greased fireproof dish, and dot with butter.
5 Bake in a hot oven (425–450°F.—Gas Mark 6–7) for about 25 minutes.

## Parmesan potatoes

cooking time about 30 minutes

**you will need for 4 servings:**

2 oz. butter
2 tablespoons flour
$\frac{3}{8}$ pint milk
6 oz. grated Parmesan cheese
seasoning
1 lb. cooked diced potatoes
paprika

1. Melt the butter and stir in the flour.
2. When well blended, add the milk and cook, stirring constantly, until mixture is thick and smooth.
3. Add 4 oz. of the cheese and stir over a low heat until the cheese has melted.
4. Remove from heat and season to taste.
5. Add the potatoes and turn mixture into a greased casserole.
6. Top with the remainder of the cheese and a sprinkling of paprika.
7. Bake in a moderately hot oven (400°F.—Gas Mark 5) for about 20 minutes or until bubbly and brown.

**Variation:**

Fry a chopped onion, and add with the cheese. Add some chopped parsley with the seasoning. Continue as above.

## Surprise cheese pie

cooking time 40 minutes

**you will need for 4 servings:**

10–12 oz. short crust pastry (see page 55)
1 egg
2 tablespoons milk
pinch salt
shake cayenne pepper
12 oz. seedless raisins
8–12 oz. grated Cheddar cheese

1. Roll out the pastry and line a 7½–8 inch deep flan ring with part of the pastry.
2. Beat egg with the milk and seasoning.
3. Put a layer of raisins in the ring, then cheese and cover with a little of the egg mixture.
4. Repeat the layers until the ingredients are used up, then cover with the remainder of the pastry.
5. Seal the edges well and decorate the top with pastry leaves.
6. Brush with a little egg white left in the shell and bake in the centre of a moderate hot oven (400°F.—Gas Mark 5) for approximately 40 minutes.
7. Serve hot or cold.

## Savoury cheese stuffed marrow

cooking time 25 minutes

**you will need for 4 servings:**

1 medium sized marrow
1 lb. shredded cabbage
½ pint cheese and onion sauce (see page 64)
8 slices toast
2 oz. grated Cheddar cheese
browned breadcrumbs
salt

1. Cut the marrow into 8 slices about 1–1½ inches thick.
2. Peel and remove seeds from each slice and partly cook in boiling salted water.
3. Cook the cabbage until tender; drain well.
4. Mix thoroughly with the cheese and onion sauce.
5. Stand the marrow rings on the toast.
6. Fill each ring with the cheese and cabbage mixture.
7. Dredge heavily with grated cheese and breadcrumbs.
8. Put under the grill for a few minutes to brown.

## Vegetable and cheese quickie

cooking time 10–15 minutes

**you will need for 4 servings:**

½ pint milk
1½ oz. butter or margarine
1½ oz. flour
¼ pint vegetable stock
seasoning
8 oz. grated Cheddar cheese
small cooked cauliflower
8 oz. cooked diced mixed vegetables (carrots, runner beans, peas, etc.)
few breadcrumbs
little extra butter

1. Make a sauce of the milk, butter or margarine and flour.
2. Add the vegetable stock, and cook until smooth.
3. Season well and stir in 6 oz. cheese and the vegetables, dividing cauliflower into pieces.
4. Put into a hot pie dish and cover with remaining cheese and breadcrumbs; dot with knobs of butter.
5. Brown under the grill.

## Savoury or herb pudding

cooking time 1½ hours

**you will need for 4 servings:**

8 oz. stale bread
2 large onions
1 teaspoon salt
8 oz. chopped suet
¼ teaspoon pepper
1 teaspoon powdered sage
1 teaspoon mixed herbs
2 beaten eggs
8 oz. fine oatmeal
dripping

1 Soak the bread in hot water for $\frac{1}{2}$ hour.
2 Drain away any unabsorbed liquid and beat smooth.
3 Boil onions in salt and water for $\frac{1}{2}$ hour and chop coarsely.
4 Mix all ingredients, adding the eggs last.
5 Melt enough dripping, in a Yorkshire pudding tin, to form a very thin layer; spread in mixture evenly.
6 Bake for about 1 hour in a moderate oven (375°F.—Gas Mark 4).
7 When cooked, cut into squares and serve with a good gravy, or sauce and cooked vegetables.

# Cheese toppings for savoury dishes

Even a toasted snack, such as mushrooms on toast, or tomatoes on toast, can be given extra food value if a slice of cheese is put on the toast before cooking, or grated cheese is sprinkled over the hot toast and toppings.

## Apple Welsh rarebit

cooking time 6–8 minutes

**you will need for 4 servings:**

8 oz. Cheddar cheese
2 oz. butter
$\frac{1}{4}$ pint brown ale
1 beaten egg
salt and freshly ground black pepper
4 rounds toast
8 rings of dessert apple
little oil
8 stuffed olives for garnish

1 Grate the cheese.
2 Put into a saucepan with the butter, ale, egg and seasoning, and stir over a low heat until smooth and thick.
3 Pile on to toast and cover with rings of apple (leaving peel on).
4 Brush apple with oil and place under grill for few minutes.
5 Garnish with stuffed olives.

## Banana Welsh rarebit No. 1

cooking time 10–15 minutes

**you will need for 4 servings:**

4 oz. Cheddar cheese
$\frac{1}{4}$ teaspoon mustard
cayenne to taste
1 tablespoon top of milk or mild beer
2 bananas
1 oz. butter
2 large slices toast

1 Grate the cheese, add mustard and cayenne, then mash together with milk or beer. (For children omit mustard and pepper.)
2 Halve peeled bananas lengthwise and then crosswise.
3 Fry in butter, turning only once.
4 Halve toast, place 2 pieces banana on each square.
5 Pile the cheese mixture on top and smooth level.
6 Place under the grill and leave until the cheese is well melted and lightly browned.

## Banana Welsh rarebit No. 2

cooking time 10 minutes

**you will need for 4 servings:**

1 lb. ripe bananas
2 oz. butter
4 large slices white bread
4 slices Cheddar cheese
gherkins or paprika to decorate

1 Mash bananas with the melted butter.
2 Toast bread on one side only, cut off crusts, cover the untoasted side with the banana spread.
3 Cover again with thin slices of cheese and place under the grill until cheese bubbles.
4 Cut into fingers, sprinkle with paprika or lay a strip of gherkin on each finger and serve hot.

## Devilled egg rarebit

cooking time 8 minutes

**you will need for 4 servings:**

2 eggs
6 oz. grated cheese
Worcestershire sauce to taste
salt and pepper
1 teaspoon flour
4 slices bread
butter

1 Beat the eggs, then add the cheese, Worcestershire sauce, salt and pepper and finally the flour; mix well together.
2 Toast the bread on one side, butter the untoasted side.
3 Spread egg and cheese mixture completely over buttered side of the bread; grill until golden brown.

## Melba toast Parmesan

cooking time few minutes

**you will need for 4 servings:**

white or protein bread
butter
grated Parmesan cheese
little paprika

1. Cut thin slices of white or protein bread and brush one side of each slice with soft butter.
2. Sprinkle with grated Parmesan cheese and a little paprika.
3. Toast slowly in a very slow oven (250°F.—Gas Mark ½) until crisp and nicely browned.

## Pineapple and cheese sizzle

cooking time 5–8 minutes

**you will need for 4 servings:**

4 slices bread
4 canned pineapple rings
6 oz. grated cheese
salt and pepper
gherkins

1. Toast bread on one side only.
2. Chop the pineapple and add to the cheese.
3. Pile this mixture on to the untoasted side of the bread.
4. Sprinkle with salt and pepper.
5. Grill until cheese is melted and sizzly.
6. Garnish with slices of gherkin and sprinkle with salt and pepper.

## Cream cheese puffs No. 1

cooking time few minutes

**you will need for 2–3 servings:**

6 oz. cream cheese
2 beaten egg yolks
1 small grated onion
2 teaspoons baking powder
slices toast or cream crackers

1. Let the cream cheese stand at room temperature and soften.
2. Blend with yolks and grated onion.
3. A few minutes before serving, add the baking powder to the cream cheese mixture, blending well.
4. Heap on to toast or cream crackers.
5. Put under grill for a minute or two until bubbly and brown.
6. Serve hot.

## Cream cheese puffs No. 2

cooking time few minutes

**you will need for 2–3 servings:**

6 oz. cream cheese
1 egg
½ teaspoon grated onion
slices bread

1. Beat cream cheese with egg until thoroughly blended, light and smooth.
2. Add onion.
3. Toast bread on one side only and spread mixture on the untoasted side.
4. Grill about 1 minute until brown and puffy.
5. Serve hot.

## Soufflé rarebit

cooking time 5–6 minutes

**you will need for 4 servings:**

1 oz. butter
2 eggs
3 oz. grated cheese
1 tablespoon milk
seasoning
4 slices bread
little parsley and sliced tomato for garnish

1. Cream butter and add beaten egg yolks, cheese, milk and seasoning.
2. Fold in stiffly beaten egg whites.
3. Toast the bread.
4. Butter, then spread over the cheese mixture.
5. Brown under the grill.
6. Garnish with parsley and tomatoes.

## Tomato cheese toasts

cooking time 15–20 minutes

**you will need for 4 servings:**

¾ oz. butter
¾ oz. flour
½ pint milk
½ teaspoon prepared mustard
dash cayenne pepper
8 oz. grated Cheddar cheese
4 slices buttered toast
4 tomatoes, skinned and sliced

1. Melt the butter in a small pan.
2. Add the flour and cook for a minute, stirring.
3. Add the milk gradually, bring to the boil and boil for a minute, stirring.
4. Add the seasoning and Cheddar cheese and stir over gentle heat until the cheese has completely melted.
5. Prepare the toast.
6. Arrange tomato slices on the toast and put under grill to heat through.
7. Pour the hot cheese sauce over and serve.

## Welsh rarebit

cooking time 10–15 minutes

**you will need for 4 servings:**

1 oz. butter
1 oz. flour
*¼ pint milk
1 teaspoon made mustard
salt
pepper
**6–8 oz. grated cheese
1 tablespoon beer or ale or Worcestershire sauce
4 large slices buttered toast

*This gives a very soft creamy Welsh rarebit. For a slightly drier Welsh rarebit and firmer texture which tends to keep a better shape, use only ⅛ pint milk.
**Cheshire or Cheddar cheese gives moderately strong result, and a Welsh rarebit that is creamier. Processed cheese gives a soft rather mild taste. By adding a little Parmesan to these cheeses you get a Welsh rarebit with a lot of flavour. Stale, rather dry cheese is often better for grating and certainly stronger in taste.

1 Heat the butter, stir in the flour and cook steadily for several minutes, then gradually add the cold milk.
2 Bring to the boil and cook until smooth and thick.
3 Add the mustard, salt, pepper, most of the cheese and the beer. Heat steadily, without boiling too quickly, until the cheese has melted.
4 Spread over the hot buttered toast, sprinkle with the remainder of the cheese and brown under a hot grill. Serve at once.

**Note:**
This Welsh rarebit mixture can be stored in covered jars for some days in a refrigerator.

**Variations:**

### Buck rarebit
Top the mixture with a poached egg.

### Celery rarebit
Arrange neat pieces of well-drained, cooked celery on the toast and coat with the Welsh rarebit mixture. Celery stock can be used instead of milk.

### Creole rarebit
Mix the rarebit mixture with fried onion, tomatoes and little sweet corn.

### Tomato rarebit
Blend the mixture with tomato juice or soup instead of milk. If using soup, add a little less flour.

### Vegetable rarebit
Mix the rarebit with few cooked well drained vegetables.

# Cheese snacks

Although the recipes that follow are really light and meant for television or cocktail snacks, they also make a sustaining dish for supper or lunch.

## Blue cheese crisps

cooking time 8–10 minutes

**you will need for 2 servings:**

2 oz. softened butter
3 oz. grated processed Cheddar cheese
1 teaspoon grated onion
3 oz. flour
4½ oz. crumbled blue cheese

1 Combine all ingredients and mix well until blended.
2 Shape into balls about ¾-inch diameter and place on an ungreased baking sheet.
3 Press down with a fork and chill for several hours.
4 Bake in a very hot oven (425°F.—Gas Mark 6) for 8–10 minutes until golden brown.

## Hot chilli Roquefort canapés

cooking time few minutes

**you will need for 2 servings or 10 tiny canapes:**

4 oz. cream cheese
1½ oz. crumbled Roquefort cheese
1 tablespoon ketchup
1¾ teaspoons chilli powder
¼ teaspoon paprika
pinch garlic powder
10 small slices bread

1 Soften the cream cheese and blend with the Roquefort cheese.
2 Add ketchup and spices and mix well.
3 Trim crusts from bread, toast slices on both sides.
4 Spread the cheese mixture on the toast and cut each piece into 3 finger-length strips.
5 Grill until browned and bubbly.
6 Sprinkle with additional paprika.

### Salted Parmesan bits

cooking time 20–25 minutes

**you will need for 4 servings or 16 canapés:**

4 oz. flour
¼ teaspoon salt
pinch pepper
3 oz. grated Parmesan cheese
3 oz. soft butter
little beaten egg or milk

1 Combine flour, salt, pepper and cheese.
2 Cut in soft butter until particles are the size of small peas.
3 Knead until a smooth ball is formed.
4 Roll out on floured board to ½-inch thickness.
5 Brush with egg or milk.
6 Cut into ½-inch rounds or cubes.
7 Place on a greased baking sheet and bake in a moderate oven (375°F.—Gas Mark 4) for 20–25 minutes.
8 Cool and store in a tightly covered container.

### Mexican cheese balls

no cooking

**you will need for 2 servings or 12 canapés:**

8 oz. cream cheese
1 tablespoon chopped green pepper
1 tablespoon chopped or minced onion
½ teaspoon salt
chopped nuts

1 Mix all ingredients, except nuts, well together.
2 Form into balls and roll in coarsely chopped nuts.
4 Serve on cocktail sticks.

### Olive cheese balls

no cooking

**you will need for 1 serving or 8 canapés:**

4 oz. cream cheese
2 oz. chopped ripe olives
1 tablespoon butter
coarsely chopped walnuts

1 Cream together thoroughly the cheese, olives and butter.
2 Form into little balls and roll in walnuts.
3 Serve on cocktail sticks.

### Parmesan canapés

cooking time few minutes

**you will need for 1 serving or 4 canapés:**

2 slices bread
finely sliced onion
¼ pint mayonnaise (see page 73)
3 tablespoons grated Parmesan cheese
extra Parmesan cheese

1 Cut bread into small rounds with a biscuit cutter.
2 Top each with a slice of onion.
3 Combine mayonnaise and cheese.
4 Place the rounds of bread on an ungreased baking sheet and top each with 1 teaspoon of cheese mixture.
5 Sprinkle with additional cheese and place under grill until golden brown.
6 Serve piping hot.

# Value of Eggs as a Main Dish

While it may look small, an egg is a complete protein food, suitable for the very young as well as adults.

A lightly boiled, poached or fried egg makes a very good meal with vegetables, and there are many variations to give added interest.

### Making omelettes

An omelette is one of the many ways of turning eggs into main meals, and the omelettes can also be varied.

1 For a substantial serving allow 2 eggs per person—and, if making omelettes for a number of people, do not try and cook too many eggs at a time. It is better to use 4–6 at the maximum, i.e. an omelette for 2–3 people, in a 7–8 inch pan. If you try to cook a larger number, the process is too slow and the eggs tend to toughen.

2 For a plain (or French) type of omelette, whisk the eggs lightly with seasoning, adding a little water if wished. Allow about 1 dessertspoon water to each egg.

3 Heat a good knob of butter or spoonful of oil in the omelette pan, put in the whisked eggs, and allow to set lightly on the bottom. Then work the mixture by loosening the omelette from the sides of the pan, at the same time tilting it so that the liquid mixture flows underneath. Continue until all liquid has set.

Fold or roll away from the handle and tip on to a hot dish. Serve immediately.

For a soufflé omelette, the whites and yolks are separated and the stiffly beaten whites folded into the beaten yolks, then seasoned. This tends to be a drier, but of course thicker and lighter omelette—and can be set without turning if given a minute or so cooking in the usual way, it is then put under a moderately hot grill, or even finished cooking in the oven if the pan handle permits.

## *Looking after your omelette pan*

If possible buy a special pan and keep it just for omelettes or omelettes and pancakes.

Don't wash it, but clean it with very soft paper (modern soft kitchen rolls are ideal for this).

Never get the butter or oil too hot so there is any possibility of anything burning in this pan.

If you are careful your pan will repay you with years of wear.

## Omelettes

cooking time — few minutes

**you will need for 3 servings:**

| | |
|---|---|
| 6 eggs | salt and pepper |
| 3 tablespoons water | 2 oz. butter |

1. Whisk eggs, water and seasoning.
2. Heat butter in a large frying pan and pour in omelette mixture.
3. Allow to set lightly on the bottom.
4. Loosen the omelette from the sides of the pan, tilting the pan from side to side, so the liquid mixture flows underneath. Continue until all the liquid is lightly set.
5. Fold or roll away from the handle.
6. Tip on to a hot dish and serve at once.

## Cornflour omelette

cooking time — 8 minutes

**you will need for 2 servings:**

| | |
|---|---|
| 2 level teaspoons cornflour | 4 eggs |
| 1–2 tablespoons water or milk | 1 tablespoon oil |
| | 1 oz. butter |

**To garnish:**

| | |
|---|---|
| 1 green or red capsicum (pepper), fresh or canned | 1 or 2 tomatoes |
| | few mushrooms |
| | butter |

1. Gently fry vegetables in butter, keep hot.
2. Mix cornflour and cold milk or water.
3. Beat eggs into this.
4. Heat oil in an omelette pan and pour mixture into it. After a few seconds of cooking, reduce heat and loosen omelette around edges of pan with a fork or palette knife, so that the uncooked mixture has a chance to cook. Continue, shaking pan occasionally, until the surface of the omelette is just creamy.
5. When omelette is ready, dot with butter, fold in three and serve with garnish of vegetables.

**Fillings for omelettes:**

### Anchovy and cheese omelette

Warm 8 oz. cottage cheese in the oven or over hot water. When omelette is cooked, spoon over the cheese on half the omelette and sprinkle with 3 or 4 chopped anchovy fillets, then fold omelette over.

### Cheese omelette

Fill with a creamy cheese sauce (see page 63) or grated cheese.

### Cheese and onion omelette

As anchovy and cheese omelette above, using 1 tablespoon finely chopped spring onion instead of anchovy fillets.

### Mixed herb omelette

Add pinch mixed herbs to the egg mixture before cooking.

### Vegetable omelette

Heat vegetables in a creamy sauce (see page 63) and put on to omelette before folding.

### Mushroom omelette

Add sliced fried mushrooms or mushrooms with white sauce (see page 63) before folding.

### Spinach omelette

Fill with hot creamed spinach.

## Cream cheese omelette

cooking time 5–6 minutes

**you will need for 2 servings:**

3 eggs
salt and pepper
1 tablespoon water
knob butter
3 oz. cream cheese

1 Beat eggs.
2 Add good pinch salt and pepper and water.
3 Put butter into omelette pan and when hot pour in mixture.
4 Leave for about 1 minute over high heat to allow bottom to set.
5 Loosen egg mixture from side to side so that the liquid egg flows underneath and cooks quickly.
6 When omelette is set, cover with cream cheese.
7 Slip palette knife under omelette and fold it away from handle of pan.
8 Turn on to hot plate.

## Fish omelette

Ingredients as omelettes (see page 27)

4–6 oz. cooked flaked fish
¼ pint cheese sauce (see recipe page 63)

Heat fish in the sauce and put on to the omelette just before folding.

## Soufflé omelettes

cooking time few minutes

**you will need for 3 servings:**

6 eggs
3 tablespoons water
salt and pepper
2 oz. butter

1 Separate the eggs.
2 Beat yolks, water and seasoning together.
3 Fold in the stiffly beaten whites.
4 Heat butter in a large frying pan and pour in omelette mixture.
5 Allow to set lightly on the bottom.
6 Loosen the omelette from sides of the pan and tilt from side to side so the liquid mixture flows underneath. Finish cooking under grill if wished firm.
7 Put filling on half and fold other half over.
8 Tip on to a hot dish and serve at once.

## Oven omelette

cooking time 25 minutes

**you will need for 4 servings:**

1 lb. cooked diced potatoes
1 large thinly sliced onion
2 oz. butter
8 eggs
1 dessertspoon chopped parsley
salt and pepper

1 Fry potatoes and onion in melted butter until golden brown.
2 Place in a shallow buttered dish, pour over beaten eggs mixed with parsley, salt and pepper.
3 Bake in a moderately hot oven (400°F.—Gas Mark 5) for 15 minutes.

## Potato omelette

cooking time 10–12 minutes

**you will need for 2 servings:**

2 oz. butter
2 small boiled diced potatoes
4 eggs
½ level teaspoon salt
pinch pepper

1 Heat the butter in the frying pan.
2 Add potatoes and cook until golden.
3 Beat the eggs slightly and season.
4 Add to the potatoes and cook quickly as for an ordinary omelette (see page 27). Take care potatoes are evenly distributed.
5 Cook further 5 minutes.
6 Fold over and serve at once.

**Variations:**

### Potato cheese omelette

Add 1 oz. finely grated Parmesan cheese to beaten eggs.

### Potato fish omelette

Add little hot cooked white fish—or chopped shrimps—to omelette just before folding.

### Tomato omelette

1 Use the plain or cornflour omelette recipes (see page 27) and for the filling, fry tomatoes in a little margarine, butter or oil.
2 Fry a little chopped onion, or crushed garlic with the tomatoes, or add grated cheese at the very last minute.

## Spanish-style omelette

cooking time few minutes

**you will need for 2 servings:**

- 1½ oz. butter
- 1 cooked diced potato
- 1 tablespoon each cooked peas, beans, carrots and mushrooms
- little chopped green pepper
- 3 eggs
- 1 tablespoon cold water
- salt and pepper
- 1 oz. grated cheese

1 Heat 1 oz. butter in pan and heat vegetables for a few minutes.
2 Beat the eggs and water together then add the hot potato, cooked peas, etc., salt and pepper.
3 Mix together.
4 Melt the rest of the butter in an omelette pan and when it is hot, but just before it begins to brown, pour in the mixture.
5 When the egg is just beginning to set at the bottom, use a fork or palette knife to draw the mixture to the middle from the sides, so that the runny egg will cook.
6 Repeat until the top is slightly runny, then sprinkle on the grated cheese and immediately place the pan under a hot grill to melt the cheese and just cook the top of the omelette.
7 Do not leave for more than a minute under the grill as the omelette will become hard.
8 Serve flat by slipping on to a plate with the cheese side up.

**Variation:**

Add 1 finely chopped onion, half a red pepper and half a green pepper, cut into thin strips. Fry with the other vegetables and continue as in the recipe above.

# Egg Dishes

## Scrambled eggs

cooking time few minutes

**you will need for 2 servings:**

- ½–1 oz. margarine or butter
- 3–4 eggs
- seasoning
- up to 2 tablespoons milk or cream, optional

1 Beat the seasoned eggs lightly.
2 Add 1 dessertspoon milk for each egg if you like a soft mixture.
3 Heat a walnut of margarine or butter, pour in the eggs and cook gently, stirring well from the bottom until the mixture starts to thicken.
4 Turn the heat very slow, continue stirring until egg mixture is lightly cooked through.

**Note:**

If you are making scrambled eggs for a very large number of people, use a rather big pan, otherwise the mixture tends to get very hard on the outside before the centre is set.
A double saucepan or basin over hot water is an easy and very efficient way of cooking scrambled eggs, and there is far less waste.

**Variations:**

### Vegetable scrambled eggs

Recipe as above. Allow approximately 8 oz. very well drained and cooked vegetables. Put these in with the hot margarine or butter and get very hot before adding the beaten eggs.

### Cheese scrambled eggs

Ingredients as above. Put in 3–4 oz. finely grated cheese when the eggs are almost set.

## Scrambled eggs with lemon and parsley

cooking time 15 minutes

**you will need for 4 servings:**

| | |
|---|---|
| 1 oz. butter | grated rind ½ lemon |
| 2 medium-sized onions | salt and pepper |
| 8 eggs | 4 slices toasted bread |
| 2 tablespoons chopped parsley | butter |
| | 4 slices cheese |

1 Melt the butter and add the finely chopped onion.
2 Cook gently for about 10 minutes, but do not let the onions brown.
3 Beat the eggs, add the chopped parsley, grated lemon rind and seasoning.
4 Add to the cooked onion and stir over a low heat until the eggs are scrambled.
5 Butter the hot toast and place thin slices of cheese on the toast.
6 Heat under grill for few minutes then pile the scrambled egg on top.
7 Serve at once.

## Scrambled eggs with peas

cooking time 20 minutes

**you will need for 2 servings:**

| | |
|---|---|
| 2 oz. butter or margarine | ⅛ teaspoon pepper |
| 1 small chopped onion | 1 tablespoon water |
| 1 lb. shelled fresh peas or large packet frozen peas | 4 eggs |
| ½ teaspoon salt | 2 tablespoons milk |
| | 2 tablespoons grated cheese |

1 Heat butter, add onion, peas, seasoning and water.
2 Cook, covered tightly and over medium heat, for 10–15 minutes or until peas are just tender.
3 Beat eggs with milk and cheese and pour over peas.
4 Cook over low heat. As eggs start to set at bottom, stir gently.
5 When cooked, serve at once.

## Soufflé scrambled eggs

1 Ingredients exactly the same as for scrambled eggs (see page 29), but separate the whites from the yolks, beat the whites stiffly and the yolks lightly with seasoning and a little milk.
2 Fold the egg whites into the yolks and cook in exactly the same way as ordinary scrambled eggs.
The mixture looks very pleasant and tends to be softer and lighter.

## English monkey

cooking time about 10 minutes

**you will need for 4 servings:**

| | |
|---|---|
| 1 oz. butter | salt, pepper |
| ½ pint milk | made mustard |
| 2 oz. soft breadcrumbs | Worcestershire sauce |
| 4 oz. grated cheese | 4 slices toast |
| 1 beaten egg | 1 tomato for garnish |

1 Heat butter, add milk and breadcrumbs.
2 When very hot, add the cheese and egg.
3 Add all seasoning.
4 Stir together until thick and creamy.
5 Pour on to toast, garnish with sliced tomato.

## Scotch woodcock

cooking time 10–15 minutes

**you will need for 4 servings:**

| | |
|---|---|
| 1½ oz. butter | 4 slices buttered toast |
| 4–6 eggs | 8 anchovy fillets and few capers for garnish |
| seasoning | |
| little milk | |

1 Heat the butter.
2 Beat the eggs with seasoning and milk.
3 Scramble slowly and, when set, pile on to buttered toast and garnish with the anchovy fillets and capers.
4 Cut toast into 8 fingers; serve as an after-dinner savoury.

## Poached eggs

cooking time few minutes

**you will need for 4 servings:**

| | |
|---|---|
| 4 eggs | 4 rounds bread |
| margarine or butter | extra butter |
| | salt |

1 Like all egg dishes, poached eggs must be served the moment they are cooked, so toast and butter the bread while they cook.
2 Crack the shells and pour the eggs into a cup or saucer.

3 If you have an egg poacher, put a piece of margarine or butter, about the size of a hazelnut, into each cup; when this is melted, carefully slide an egg into the cup, adding a pinch of salt if wished.
4 Put on the lid and allow the water in the pan underneath to boil steadily for about 3½–4 minutes.
5 Slide the egg on to the buttered toast and serve.

**Alternative method:**

1 Put a small piece of margarine or butter into an old cup and stand it in a pan of boiling water until fat melts. Pour in egg, put a lid on saucepan and cook as before.
Or the following method is preferred by many people since it gives a lighter result:
2 Bring a good ½ pint of water to the boil in either a saucepan or frying pan.
3 Add 1 dessertspoon vinegar if wished, as it prevents the whites from spreading. Put in good pinch of salt.
4 Break eggs and slide into the boiling water, leave for about 3 minutes, or until whites are set.
5 Insert spoon or fish slice, drain the eggs carefully and put on prepared toast.

## Poached eggs Florentine

cooking time 20 minutes

**you will need for 4 servings:**

4 eggs
little butter or margarine
1 lb. spinach
½ pint cheese sauce (see page 63)

1 Cook the spinach until just tender, adding seasoning and little or no water.
2 Either sieve or chop finely, adding a small amount of butter or margarine. Arrange in a shallow dish.
3 Top with the poached eggs and cheese sauce; put for 1 minute under the grill until the sauce bubbles.
4 Serve at once.

**Variation:**

### Poached egg and spinach mornay

Recipe as above, but top the cheese sauce with a few breadcrumbs and grated cheese to give a slightly crisp top.

## Fried eggs

Heat a little butter or oil in a pan and, when hot, add the eggs carefully.
Cook until just set, or as preferred.

## Eggs on apples and onions

cooking time 25 minutes

**you will need for 4 servings:**

4 medium-sized onions
2 oz. butter
8 eggs
2 medium-sized cooking apples
salt and pepper

1 Roughly chop the onions.
2 Melt the butter in a large frying pan, add the onions, cover and cook slowly for 5 minutes. They must not brown, but should be almost transparent.
3 Meanwhile, core the apples, but do not peel.
4 Cut into thin slices, and add to the onions.
5 Continue cooking slowly for a further 15 minutes.
6 Make an even bed and season with salt and pepper.
7 Break the eggs on top, cover and cook slowly until just done—about 5 minutes.

**Note:**
You will probably find it better to divide apple and onion mixture and cook 4 eggs at a time.

## Sweetcorn and buttered fried eggs

cooking time 10–15 minutes

**you will need for 4 servings:**

2½ oz. butter
½ oz. flour
¼ pint milk
1 can sweetcorn (or large packet frozen sweetcorn)
4 oz. grated cheese
seasoning
8 eggs

1 Melt ½ oz. butter and stir in the flour.
2 Cook for 1 minute over a low heat and stir in the milk.
3 Bring to the boil and cook gently for 2 minutes.
4 Add the cooked sweetcorn and cheese to the sauce and keep hot, season well.
5 Fry the eggs in remaining butter.
6 To serve, place the sweetcorn mixture in the bottom of a hot dish, the fried eggs on top, and serve with jacket potatoes.

## Fried eggs à la cubana

cooking time 10 minutes

**you will need for 4 servings:**

8 eggs
3 tablespoons olive oil
8 oz. hot cooked rice
4 bananas
seasoned flour
hot tomato sauce

1 Fry the eggs in the olive oil, one or two at a time, until just firm, the yolks still soft.
2 Arrange cooked eggs over top of rice.
3 Roll bananas, each cut in half lengthwise, in the flour.
4 Fry in remaining oil in pan.
5 Serve two fried banana halves for each serving.
6 Hot tomato sauce may be served separately.

## Asparagus eggs

cooking time 20 minutes

**you will need for 4 servings:**

1 medium can asparagus
pinch grated nutmeg, cayenne pepper, castor sugar
½ oz. butter
¼ pint milk
4 eggs
1 oz. grated cheese

1 Drain asparagus thoroughly.
2 Mash in a basin.
3 Stir in nutmeg, cayenne pepper and sugar.
4 Turn into a saucepan and add butter and milk, season well.
5 Simmer gently, stirring constantly, for a minute or two.
6 Line a shallow buttered fireproof dish with the mixture.
7 Break eggs carefully into dish.
8 Sprinkle with cheese and bake in a hot oven (450°F.—Gas Mark 7) for 10–15 minutes.

## Banana and egg curry

cooking time 15–20 minutes

**you will need for 4 servings:**

2 oz. butter
2 small sliced onions
1 dessert apple
½ teaspoon salt
2 oz. sultanas (washed)
1 oz. flour
½ pint milk
1–2 teaspoons curry powder
¼ pint water
2 bananas
4 hard-boiled eggs
chutney
cooked rice

1 Melt the butter in a heavy frying pan.
2 Fry the onion until transparent.
3 Add the peeled, diced apple, salt and sultanas.
4 Sprinkle with flour and stir.
5 Blend curry powder (amount according to taste) with the milk and water.
6 Add to the mixture and stir over heat until thick.
7 Add the bananas, peeled and cut into 1½ inch pieces, and cook slowly for 5 minutes.
8 Add quartered hard-boiled eggs.
9 Serve with chutney and cooked rice.

## Creamed curried eggs

cooking time 15 minutes

**you will need for 4 servings:**

2 oz. margarine
½–1 tablespoon curry powder
1 small onion
1 oz. flour
¼ pint milk
⅛ pint cream or top of milk
few raisins
4 oz. cooked rice
8 hard-boiled eggs

1 Heat margarine, add curry powder, and fry chopped onions in this.
2 Stir in flour, then gradually add milk. Cook until thickened.
3 Stir in the cream, raisins and, just before serving, add the quartered hard-boiled eggs. Serve in border of cooked rice.

**Note:**
The rice mixture can be varied by frying chopped onion and/or red and green peppers in margarine, then adding to rice.

## Curried eggs

cooking time approximately 45 minutes

**you will need for 4 servings:**

**For sauce:**
2 oz. margarine
1 chopped onion
1 chopped apple
1 tablespoon curry powder
1 tablespoon flour
1 pint stock or water
4 hard-boiled eggs
squeeze lemon juice
1 dessertspoon desiccated coconut
1 tablespoon dried fruit
1 teaspoon sugar
1 dessertspoon chutney
seasoning
rice
chutney

1 Heat the margarine, fry the onion and apple until soft.
2 Stir in the curry powder and flour and cook for several minutes.
3 Add liquid and bring to the boil.
4 Stir in all the other ingredients and simmer for about 35 minutes.
5 Cut the hard-boiled eggs into quarters and

heat in the sauce, for about 5 minutes—do not over-cook otherwise they will become tough.

6 Serve in a ring of boiled rice and top with chutney.

## Devilled eggs creole

cooking time 40–45 minutes

**you will need for 4 servings:**

1 small onion
1 small green pepper
1 stick celery
1 oz. butter
2 oz. chopped mushrooms
6 oz. rice
½ pint plus 2 tablespoons stock or water
seasoning

**For sauce:**

1 oz. butter
1 oz. flour
½ pint tomato juice
1 rounded teaspoon made mustard
salt
1 teaspoon Worcestershire sauce
pinch brown sugar
4 hard-boiled eggs

1 Chop or coarsely mince onion, green pepper and celery.
2 Heat butter, fry the onion, pepper and celery for 5 minutes without browning.
3 Add mushrooms and rice and cook gently for 4 minutes.
4 Add stock and cover pan and cook for 20 minutes until no moisture remains.
5 Season to taste.
6 Meanwhile, make the sauce by melting the butter and stirring in the flour.
7 Cook for 2 minutes and remove from heat.
8 Gradually add tomato juice and reheat till sauce thickens, stirring all the time.
9 Add remaining ingredients and simmer gently for 5–10 minutes.
10 Add salt to taste.
11 Turn rice mixture into bottom of a warm serving dish.
12 Arrange halved eggs on top and coat with a little sauce.
13 Serve remaining sauce separately.

## Devilled eggs Angostura

no cooking

**you will need for 4 servings:**

6 hard-boiled eggs
mayonnaise (see page 73)
1 teaspoon Angostura bitters

1 Slice hard-boiled eggs in half lengthwise and remove yolks.
2 Put yolks through a sieve.
3 Add mayonnaise to make desired consistency and add Angostura bitters to mixture.
4 Re-stuff whites with filling and chill.

## Soufflé sandwich

cooking time 18 minutes

**you will need for 4 servings:**

4 slices bread
4 slices cheese, processed or Cheddar
4 eggs
2 tablespoons salad cream
salt and pepper
2 tomatoes

1 Toast the bread on one side.
2 Cover each untoasted side with slice of cheese.
3 Separate the eggs.
4 Add the salad cream and seasoning to the yolks and beat until light.
5 Whisk the whites until very stiff.
6 Fold the yolk mixture into the whites.
7 Pile on top of the cheese and bake in a moderate oven (375°F.—Gas Mark 4) near top until puffy and brown—about 15 minutes.

## Egg and vegetable cutlets

cooking time 8–10 minutes

**you will need for 4 servings:**

4–5 hard-boiled eggs
8–12 oz. diced and cooked mixed vegetables
1 oz. breadcrumbs
¼ pint thick white sauce (see page 63)
seasoning

**To coat:**

egg
crisp breadcrumbs
fat or oil for frying

1 Chop eggs.
2 Mix with other ingredients and form into 4 or 8 small cutlet shapes.
3 Brush with beaten egg, roll in breadcrumbs.
4 Fry in hot fat or oil until crisp and golden brown. Serve hot or cold.

**Variations:**

### Egg and cheese cutlets

Use 4 oz. grated cheese and 2 oz. breadcrumbs; omit vegetables.

### Egg and rice cutlets

Use 3 oz. cooked rice (i.e. approx. 1½ oz. uncooked rice) instead of breadcrumbs and vegetables. Season well and add mixed herbs for flavour.

### Tomato egg cutlets

Recipe as on page 33, but use tomato sauce (see page 65) in place of white sauce.

### Savoury cutlets

cooking time 15 minutes

**you will need for 4 servings:**

| | |
|---|---|
| 1 lb. mashed potatoes | seasoning |
| 4 hard-boiled eggs | 1 beaten egg |
| $\frac{1}{4}$ pint thick onion sauce (panada consistency) (see page 63) | 1 packet dry sage and onion stuffing or crisp breadcrumbs |
| | fat for frying |

1 Mix together the potato, chopped eggs, onion sauce and seasoning.
2 Divide into portions, shape them into rounds, and coat each one with the beaten egg and stuffing or breadcrumbs.
3 Fry on both sides until golden brown.
4 Serve hot or cold, with a salad.

### Egg cutlets Portuguése

cooking time 20 minutes

**you will need for 4 servings:**

| | |
|---|---|
| 1 large onion | 2 oz. breadcrumbs |
| 2 large tomatoes | 4–5 hard-boiled eggs |
| 2 oz. mushrooms | seasoning |
| **To coat:** | |
| beaten egg | fat or oil for frying |
| crisp breadcrumbs | |

1 Skin and peel the tomatoes and onion, chop very finely.
2 Wash and chop the mushrooms.
3 Fry all the vegetables in the fat until a soft purée. Do not let them discolour. Stir in the breadcrumbs, the chopped hard-boiled egg and season well.
4 Allow the mixture to cool, then form into 4–8 small cutlet shapes. Brush with beaten egg.
5 Roll in crisp breadcrumbs and fry in hot fat or oil until crisp and golden brown.
6 Serve hot or cold.

### Savoury egg custard

cooking time 35–45 minutes

**you will need for 2 servings:**

| | |
|---|---|
| yolks 2 eggs or 1 egg | $\frac{1}{4}$ pint milk |
| $\frac{1}{8}$ pint beef tea, or water and yeast extract | seasoning |

1 Beat the yolks, add the beef tea, milk and seasoning.
2 Pour into a greased pie dish. Stand the dish in another containing water and cook in the middle of a very moderate oven (350°F.—Gas Mark 3) for 35–40 minutes until just set.

**Variations:**

### Cheese savoury custard

Add 1–2 oz. grated cheese to the egg yolks.

### Herb custard

Add a good pinch of mixed herbs and about a teaspoon of chopped fried onions.

### Vegetable egg custard

Add 4 oz. cooked well drained vegetables to the egg yolks.

# Nut Dishes

### *Value of nuts as a main dish*

Nuts are a very satisfying food as vegetarians can prove, and while many people are used to eating them as a snack or part of a dessert, nuts can form the basis of an enjoyable meal. Because they are fairly dry when cooked, nuts lend themselves to dishes like Croquettes where the frying preserves the maximum of moisture, and they are excellent with a good sauce.

### Chestnut croquettes No. 1

cooking time 30–35 minutes

**you will need for 4 servings:**

| | |
|---|---|
| 1 lb. chestnuts | seasoning |
| water to cover | 1 beaten egg |
| $1\frac{1}{2}$–2 oz. breadcrumbs | very little milk |
| 2 tablespoons very finely chopped celery | $\frac{1}{2}$ pint cheese or tomato sauce (see pages 63, 65) |

1 Slit the chestnut skins, boil in water for 15 minutes and then skin.

2 Put into fresh water and simmer for a further 15 minutes until soft enough to rub through a sieve.
3 Mix the nut purée, breadcrumbs, celery, seasoning, egg and enough milk to bind. Form into croquettes and put into hot entrée dish, then pour over the hot sauce, allowing about 15 minutes in a hot oven (425°F.—Gas Mark 6), depending on size of croquettes.

## Chestnut croquettes No. 2

cooking time 50–60 minutes

**you will need for 4 servings:**

1 lb. chestnuts
4 oz. breadcrumbs
2 tablespoons finely chopped celery
seasoning
1 beaten egg
little milk

1 Slit the chestnut skins and boil in water for 15 minutes.
2 Remove skins and put into fresh water and simmer for a further 15 minutes.
3 Rub through a sieve.
4 Mix the chestnut purée, breadcrumbs, celery, seasoning, egg and enough milk to bind.
5 Form into croquettes and bake in the oven (425°F.—Gas Mark 6) or fry in hot fat until crisp.

## Chestnuts, braised

cooking time 1 hour 25 minutes

**you will need for 4 servings:**

1 lb. chestnuts
1 onion
few pieces celery
$\frac{3}{4}$ pint brown sauce (see page 64)
seasoning
crisp toast or fried bread, and grated cheese for garnish

1 Make a small split in the skin of each nut and put into boiling water. Boil for 10–15 minutes, then drain and skin while still hot.
2 Put the nuts into a casserole, add finely shredded onion and celery. Sprinkle with salt and pepper.
3 Pour over sauce and put lid on casserole.
4 Cook in the middle of a very moderate oven (350°F.—Gas Mark 3) for 1 hour. Take the lid off casserole after 30 minutes to allow sauce to thicken.
5 Serve piping hot, garnished with toast or fried bread and a generous sprinkling of cheese.

## Chestnut cutlets

cooking time 35 minutes

**you will need for 4 servings:**

1 lb. chestnuts
2 oz. breadcrumbs
seasoning
**To coat:**
egg
breadcrumbs
1 beaten egg
very little milk
oil or fat to fry

1 Slit the chestnut skins and boil in water for 10–15 minutes and then skin while warm.
2 Put into fresh water and simmer for 15 minutes until soft enough to rub through a sieve.
3 Mix chestnut purée, breadcrumbs, seasoning, egg and milk to bind. Form into cutlet shapes.
4 Coat with beaten egg and breadcrumbs, and fry in hot oil or fat until crisp and golden.

**Variations:**

### Braised cutlets

Fry for 1 minute only to set coating, then cover with tomato sauce (see page 65) and bake in a moderate oven (375°F.—Gas Mark 4) for 20 minutes.

### Herbed chestnut cutlets

Add 1–2 teaspoons mixed chopped fresh herbs to mixture or $\frac{1}{2}$ teaspoon dried herbs.

## Nut curry

cooking time 45 minutes

**you will need for 4 servings:**

2 oz. vegetarian fat
2 large onions
1 small apple
1 tablespoon curry powder
1 level tablespoon flour
1 pint water
little yeast extract
8 oz. nuts—Brazils, cashew or peanuts
1 teaspoon sugar
good pinch salt and pepper
1 teaspoon jam
few drops lemon juice
3 oz. boiled rice

1 Heat the fat, fry the onions and apple until just soft.
2 Stir in the curry powder and flour and add water flavoured with the yeast extract.
3 Bring to the boil and cook until thickened.
4 Add the nuts and all the other ingredients, except rice.
5 Heat well and pour over the hot rice.
6 Serve at once.

## Peanut roast

cooking time approximately 1¼ hours

**you will need for 4 servings:**

8 oz. peanuts
2 oz. vegetarian fat
2 onions
2 large tomatoes
1 small peeled, cored and chopped apple
1 oz. oatmeal or breadcrumbs
1 teaspoon sage
seasoning
1 beaten egg
little milk

1 Chop or grind peanuts.
2 Heat the fat; fry the onions, skinned tomatoes and apple until soft.
3 Add the peanuts, oatmeal or breadcrumbs, sage and seasoning.
4 Bind with the egg and enough milk to give a fairly moist consistency.
5 Press into a greased medium-sized loaf tin and cover with greased paper.
6 Bake in the centre of a moderately hot oven (350°F.—Gas Mark 3) for 45 minutes–1 hour.

## Nut cutlets

cooking time about 15 minutes

**you will need for 4 servings:**

Ingredients as for Peanut roast (see above).

Follow instructions 1 to 4 for Peanut roast, then:

1 Form into cutlets, brush with beaten egg and breadcrumbs.
2 Fry, or bake in the centre of a moderately hot oven (350°F.—Gas Mark 3) for 15 minutes, until crisp and brown.

**Variations:**

### Brazils

Chop.

### Cashew nuts

Chop.

### Chestnuts

Slit skins. Boil for few minutes—skin, then simmer until tender.

### Peanuts

Skin and chop.

## Nut roast

cooking time 45–60 minutes

**you will need for 4 servings:**

*8 oz. mixed nuts or nutmeat
2 oz. fat
2 chopped onions
2 good sized tomatoes
1 teaspoon sage
1 small apple—peeled, cored and chopped
1 oz. oatmeal or breadcrumbs
seasoning
1 egg

1 Either chop or grind the nuts.
2 Heat the fat; fry the onions, skinned tomatoes and apple until soft, add to the nuts (together with the oatmeal or breadcrumbs, sage and seasoning) and bind with the egg. It gives a more moist loaf if a little milk or water (flavoured with yeast extract) is added with the egg.
3 Continue as for Lentil roast (see page 38).

*Basic recipe: nutmeat obtainable from Health Food Stores.

**Variations:**

### Brazils

Chop.

### Cashew nuts

Chop.

### Chestnuts

Slit skins—boil for few minutes—skin, then simmer until tender.

## Chilli walnuts

cooking time about 10 minutes

**you will need for 2 servings:**

8 oz. shelled walnuts
little butter or margarine
chilli powder
salt

1 Lightly sauté walnuts in butter, stirring occasionally.
2 When the nuts are crisp and lightly browned, dust liberally with chilli powder and salt.
3 Place on absorbent kitchen paper to drain.
4 Serve with crisp green salad.

## Chilli Brazils

Ingredients as Chilli walnuts, substituting Brazil nuts for walnuts.

## Savoury cobblers

cooking time 10–15 minutes

**you will need for 4 servings:**

4 oz. minced onion
butter or margarine
8 oz. cobnuts
4 oz. breadcrumbs
1 dessertspoon lemon juice
2 teaspoons chopped parsley
salt and pepper
2 beaten eggs
lemon slices for garnish

1 Gently fry onion in butter until soft.
2 Mix together the nuts, onion, breadcrumbs, lemon juice, parsley, salt, pepper and eggs.
3 Shape into patties and fry in butter until golden.
4 Drain on clean paper, garnish with lemon.

## Macaroni and walnut casserole

cooking time 40–45 minutes

**you will need for 4 servings:**

3 oz. quick cooking macaroni
12 oz. tomatoes
2 teaspoons grated onions
seasoning
2 bay leaves
2 oz. grated Parmesan cheese
4 oz. shelled walnuts

1 Cook macaroni as directed on the packet.
2 Drain thoroughly.
3 Put skinned sliced tomatoes into a saucepan with the onion, seasoning and bay leaves.
4 Cook very slowly, stirring well to begin with, until a thick purée.
5 Remove bay leaves and grease a medium-sized pie dish.
6 Place a layer of macaroni in dish, then a layer of tomatoes, a sprinkling of cheese and the nuts.
7 Cover with layers of macaroni, tomato and cheese and bake in the centre of a moderately hot oven (400°F.—Gas Mark 5) for 25 minutes.

# Pulse Dishes

### *Value of peas, beans, lentils as a main dish*

These foods, commonly known as the "pulses", are tasty, sustaining and nutritious.

In all the recipes, the cooking time given is the minimum to soften the lentils or whatever the basic food may be. You may find, for quality varies, that you need just a little longer to get them very tender, so always allow plenty of time.

Fresh peas and beans are also a second-class protein, so if served with a cheese or an egg sauce, they make a complete protein dish.

## Lentil curry

cooking time 1½ hours

**you will need for 4 servings:**

8 oz. lentils
2 oz. dripping or margarine
2 large chopped onions
1 tablespoon curry powder
1 small peeled, cored and chopped apple
1 teaspoon sugar
good pinch salt and pepper
1 teaspoon jam
few drops lemon juice
3 oz. boiled rice

1 Soak the lentils for a few hours, then simmer in cold water in which they were soaked, until just soft. Try to keep them whole.
2 Fry the onions and apple in fat until soft.
3 Mix in all other ingredients, except the rice.
4 Heat well, then pour over the boiled rice.

## Lentil cutlets

cooking time 1¼ hours

**you will need for 4 servings:**

8 oz. lentils
2 oz. vegetarian fat or oil for frying
2 chopped onions
2 large tomatoes
2 oz. breadcrumbs
1 small peeled, cored and chopped apple
1 teaspoon sage
seasoning
1 egg

**To coat:**
2 oz. breadcrumbs
little beaten egg

1 Soak the lentils overnight in cold water.
2 Cook in the same water until they are soft and the water absorbed.
3 Beat until smooth.
4 Heat the fat and fry the onions, skinned tomatoes, and apple until quite soft.
5 Add to the lentils, together with the breadcrumbs, sage, seasoning.
6 Bind with the egg and form into cutlet shapes.
7 Roll in breadcrumbs after brushing with a little beaten egg and fry or bake in oven (425°F.—Gas Mark 6) until crisp and brown.

## Haricot bean curry

Substitute haricot beans for lentils (see page 37).

These take a good 2–2½ hours to get tender, and because they are more solid than lentils, it will be a better curry if about ¼ pint of vegetable stock is added to the fried onions and apple.

## Lentil roast

cooking time 1 hour 45 minutes–2 hours

**you will need for 4 servings:**

Ingredients as for Lentil cutlets (see page 37).

Follow instructions 1 to 5, then bind mixture with egg:

1 Press into a greased loaf tin and cover with greased paper.
2 Bake in the centre of a moderately hot oven (375°F.—Gas Mark 4) for 45–60 minutes.
3 Serve with brown gravy and vegetables.

## Split pea roast

Use split peas in place of lentils in the roast. You may find they need rather longer to cook.

## Haricot bean roast

Use haricot beans in place of lentils.

Allow 2½ hours cooking time, and if wished rub through a sieve before mixing with the other ingredients.

Because haricot beans have a rather less definite flavour, seasoning can be increased, adding plenty of mixed herbs.

## Bean cutlets

Ingredients as Lentil cutlets (see page 37), but use cooked haricot beans in place of the lentils.

These will probably take about 2½ hours to become tender and if the skins appear a little tough, rub through a sieve before using.

## Lentil loaf

cooking time 1 hour 45 minutes–2 hours

Recipe as for Lentil cutlets (see page 37), using 1 oz. oatmeal or breadcrumbs in place of the 2 oz. breadcrumbs. After binding with the egg, press into a greased loaf tin and cover with greased paper. Bake in the centre of a moderately hot oven (400°F.—Gas Mark 5) for 45 minutes–1 hour.

## Bean-cheese croquettes

cooking time 8 minutes

**you will need for 4 servings:**

1 egg
large can baked beans in tomato sauce
2 oz. grated Cheddar cheese
1 tablespoon finely chopped onion
1 teaspoon salt
dash pepper
3 oz. soft breadcrumbs
vegetarian oil or margarine for frying

1 Thoroughly mix all ingredients except breadcrumbs and oil or margarine.
2 Shape into small round balls and sprinkle with breadcrumbs.
3 Brown in heated oil or margarine and serve with tomato sauce (see page 65).

## Bean and rice fritters

cooking time 10–15 minutes

**you will need for 4 servings:**

4 oz. self-raising flour (with plain flour, add 1½ teaspoons baking powder
½ teaspoon salt
pinch pepper and paprika
2 eggs
½ pint milk
8 oz. cooked chopped French or runner beans
3–4 oz. cooked rice
1 teaspoon chopped onion
cooking fat

1 Sift together flour, salt, pepper and paprika.
2 Add beaten eggs and milk, mix until smooth.
3 Stir in beans, rice and onion.
4 Heat fat in a frying pan until smoking slightly and drop tablespoons of the mixture into the fat, which must be fairly deep.
5 Cook until golden brown and drain on absorbent paper.

## Bean curry

cooking time 40 minutes

**you will need for 4 servings:**

- 6 oz. long grain rice
- 1 large onion
- 1 green pepper
- 4 oz. cooking apples
- 1 oz. margarine
- 1 level dessertspoon curry powder
- ½ pint water
- salt and pepper
- pinch sugar
- 2 16-oz. cans curried beans and sultanas

**To garnish:**

- chopped parsley
- lemon butterflies

1. Wash and cook the rice in rapidly boiling salted water until tender—approximately 15 minutes.
2. Strain and rinse well with hot water to separate the grains.
3. Spread on a large flat greased dish. Cover with a cloth and dry in a cool oven or warming drawer of oven.
4. Chop onion, pepper and peeled, cored apples.
5. Fry onion in margarine until golden brown; add the curry powder and fry for a further 2 minutes.
6. Add the apple, green pepper and water; season with salt, pepper and sugar. Simmer for 20 minutes.
7. Turn the curried beans into the pan and simmer for a further 5 minutes.
8. Arrange a border of rice around a serving dish and place the curry in the centre.
9. Garnish with parsley and lemon.

**Note:**

If using ordinary beans then fry 1–2 teaspoons curry powder with onion—Step 5—and add 1–2 oz. sultanas at Step 7.

## Beans with cheese and relish

cooking time 30 minutes

**you will need for 4 servings:**

- 1 large can baked beans in tomato sauce
- 4 oz. grated cheese
- 2 oz. chopped gherkins

**To garnish:**

- gherkins
- chutney

1. Combine ingredients in casserole.
2. Bake for 30 minutes in moderate oven (375°F —Gas Mark 4) until hot and cheese is melted.
3. Serve with sliced gherkin and chutney.

## Haricot potato pie

cooking time approximately 45 minutes

**you will need for 4 servings:**

- 2 oz. vegetarian margarine
- 3 sliced tomatoes
- 1 sliced onion (optional)
- ½ pint cheese sauce (see page 63)
- 4 oz. cooked haricot beans
- 2 hard-boiled eggs
- seasoning
- 2 oz. grated cheese
- 1 lb. cooked potatoes

1. Heat margarine; fry the tomatoes and onion.
2. Add cheese sauce, beans, sliced hard-boiled eggs and seasoning.
3. Put alternate layers of bean mixture, sprinkling of the cheese and neatly sliced potato into pie dish, ending with potatoes.
4. Top with grated cheese.
5. Cook for about 35 minutes in a moderate oven (375°F.—Gas Mark 4) until piping hot.

## Peas and carrots de luxe

cooking time 40–45 minutes

**you will need for 4 servings:**

- 1 packet frozen peas or 1 lb. fresh peas
- 1 packet frozen carrots or 1 lb. fresh carrots
- 2 oz. butter or margarine
- 2 oz. chopped onion
- 1½ oz. flour
- ½ teaspoon salt
- ¼ teaspoon dry mustard
- pinch pepper
- little milk
- 1 tablespoon chopped parsley
- 6 oz. grated Cheddar cheese
- 4 oz. fresh breadcrumbs

1. Cook peas and carrots until tender; drain, reserving cooking liquid.
2. Preheat oven to 350°F.—Gas Mark 3. Fry onion in butter until golden—about 3 minutes. Remove from heat.
3. Stir in flour, salt, mustard and pepper to make a smooth mixture.
4. Measure reserved liquid: add milk to measure ½ pint.
5. Gradually stir into flour mixture and bring to boil stirring, when mixture will be thickened and smooth.
6. Reduce heat and add parsley and cheese; cook, stirring over low heat until cheese is melted.
7. Spoon peas and carrots into casserole and pour cheese sauce over. Sprinkle with breadcrumbs.
8. Bake, uncovered for 20 minutes or until crumbs are golden.

## Rice and bean creole

cooking time 1–1½ hours

**you will need for 4 servings:**

3 oz. uncooked rice
1 lb. runner or French beans
1 medium onion
1 small green pepper
12 oz. tomatoes
1¼ pints water
1 teaspoon yeast extract
¼ teaspoon pepper
2 teaspoons salt
little butter or margarine

1 Sprinkle half the rice in the bottom of a large greased baking dish.
2 Cover with half the shredded beans, half the chopped onion and half the chopped green pepper.
3 Chop tomatoes and heat with the water, yeast extract and seasonings.
4 Put half tomato mixture over the layer of pepper in baking dish and dot with butter.
5 Repeat layers once more and bake in the centre of a very moderate oven (350°F.—Gas Mark 3) for 1–1½ hours until rice is tender and beans cooked.

## Savoury bean fritters

cooking time 2¼ hours

**you will need for 4 servings:**

12 oz. dried haricot beans
water
1 teaspoon ginger
2 tablespoons vegetarian oil
1 onion
1 clove garlic
1–2 teaspoons salt
pinch chilli powder
¼ teaspoon black pepper
oil for frying

1 Soak beans overnight in cold water to cover.
2 Bring to boil in same water and add ginger.
3 Cook covered, over low heat for 2 hours or until very tender. Avoid adding additional water, if possible. When beans are tender you should have no water left.
4 Gently mash beans with a potato masher so that they are fully crushed and smooth.
5 Heat the oil in a large heavy pan.
6 Add the finely chopped onion and garlic and cook for 3 minutes.
7 Add mashed beans and salt, chilli powder and pepper.
8 Heat for 5–10 minutes, stirring, until thoroughly hot.
9 Mixture should be dry—taste for seasoning.
10 Form into flat cakes when cool.
11 Heat enough oil in frying pan to give ½-inch depth.
12 Fry bean cakes until brown.
13 Drain on absorbent paper.

## Sweet 'n sour beans

cooking time 1 minute

**you will need for 4 servings:**

⅛ pint cider vinegar
½ teaspoon dry mustard
1 teaspoon salt
1 tablespoon sugar
8 oz. cooked haricot beans
2 tablespoons vegetarian oil
½ sliced onion
rings raw onion and green or red pepper and sprigs parsley for garnish

1 Heat vinegar, dry mustard, salt and sugar for 1 minute.
2 Cool and add salad oil.
3 Mix cold beans thoroughly in this marinade.
4 Toss with the sliced onion.
5 Garnish with parsley and onion and pepper rings.

# Pasta Dishes

## *Value of Pasta*

The pasta foods, i.e. spaghetti, ravioli, macaroni, etc. are extremely good ways of serving meals without meat, for they provide really substantial dishes at small cost.
The dishes can be served with various sauces, accompanied by grated cheese.

## *Cooking tips*

Whichever type of pasta you choose, it is important to remember the following rules:—

1. Always put the spaghetti, macaroni, etc. into boiling salted water. Otherwise it will sink to the bottom of the pan, stick, and be heavy.
2. Allow sufficient water so the pasta boils with plenty of movement. Generally speaking, you need 2 pints of water to each 4 oz. of pasta.
3. Do not overcook, because overcooked pasta loses its flavour and texture.
4. Drain well before serving, and also you can pour boiling water over the pasta to get rid of the starchy texture.

## *Serving*

### Noodles

Noodles are generally a form of pasta which incorporates egg. There are various types—long ribbon noodles, squares, shell shapes, etc. Noodles are delicious cooked and served with the following:—

Anchovy sauce (see page 63).

Cheese sauce—and perhaps topped with extra grated cheese (see page 63).

Tomato sauce—and served with extra grated cheese (see page 65).

### Macaroni

The most popular way to serve macaroni is in a Macaroni cheese (see this page), but it is also excellent with a tomato or meat sauce. Since this book does not cover meat recipes, the easiest way of having a meat sauce is to heat a can of oxtail or kidney soup.

Macaroni is also very good topped with scrambled or poached eggs.

### Spaghetti

Spaghetti is at its best served with a really good tomato sauce (see page 65) and plenty of grated cheese, preferably Parmesan. Try it tossed in butter and chopped parsley, and served with plenty of grated cheese.

It is also delicious if a curry sauce (see page 64) is poured over and garnished with slices of hard-boiled egg.

### Cheese noodles

cooking time approximately 45 minutes

**you will need for 4 servings:**

- 6 oz. noodles
- 6–8 oz. cream cheese
- 1 oz. grated Parmesan cheese
- 2 oz. butter
- 2 tablespoons parsley
- 1 small sliced onion
- 3 beaten eggs
- seasoning

1. Cook the noodles in salted water until tender.
2. Strain well and add the cheese and all other ingredients, seasoning to taste.
3. Bake in a greased casserole for approximately 30 minutes in the centre of a moderate oven (375°F.—Gas Mark 4).

### Macaroni cheese

cooking time 40–45 minutes

**you will need for 4 servings:**

- 4 oz. quick cooking macaroni
- 1 oz. butter
- 1 oz. flour
- ½ pint milk
- seasoning
- 8 oz. grated Cheddar cheese

1. Cook macaroni as directed and drain.
2. Melt butter.
3. Add flour and cook for a few seconds.
4. Gradually stir in the milk and bring to the boil.
5. Boil for 2 minutes and season well.
6. Put alternate layers of cheese and macaroni in greased pie dish and cover with the sauce.
7. Sprinkle with a little cheese.
8. Bake in the centre of a moderate oven (375°F.—Gas Mark 4) for 15–20 minutes until lightly browned.

**Variations:**

#### Thick macaroni

When using thick macaroni, it needs rather longer cooking and it is better to allow approximately ¾ pint of white sauce to 4 oz. macaroni.

#### Mushroom macaroni cheese

Put alternate layers of macaroni, chopped fried mushrooms and grated cheese into the dish and cover with the sauce, or use mushroom soup in place of white sauce.

#### Tomato macaroni cheese

Substitute ½ pint tomato sauce (see page 65) for white sauce with thick macaroni. Or use ½ pint tomato soup instead of the sauce.

## Ten-minute macaroni cheese

**you will need for 4 servings:**

4 oz. quick-cooking macaroni
1 oz. butter or margarine
seasoning
approximately ¼ pint milk
8 oz. grated cheese

1 Cook the macaroni in boiling salted water for approximately 7 minutes.
2 Strain and mix with the other ingredients.
3 Heat for 2 or 3 minutes only and then serve at once.

**Variations:**

The mixture can be topped with breadcrumbs, grated cheese, and browned under the grill.

**Variation:**

Follow the recipe above, but add 2 skinned and chopped tomatoes to the sauce.

## Macaroni hot pot

cooking time 25 minutes

**you will need for 4 servings:**

8 oz. macaroni
2 oz. olive oil
1 onion
1 green pepper (optional)
4 oz. large mushrooms
2 large tomatoes
seasoning
pinch mixed herbs
squeeze lemon juice
1 large can curried or haricot beans
1 onion, raw for garnish
2 sliced tomatoes for garnish

1 Cook macaroni in boiling salted water for 7–12 minutes.
2 Heat oil; fry finely chopped onion, pepper cut into strips, sliced mushrooms, peeled and chopped tomatoes, for about 10 minutes.
3 Add seasonings, herbs and lemon juice.
4 Add beans and mix with drained macaroni; heat thoroughly.
5 Top with raw onion slices and tomato rings and serve.

## Spaghetti and mushroom loaf

cooking time approximately 1 hour

**you will need for 4 servings:**

4 oz. spaghetti
2 oz. margarine
1 small onion
2 large tomatoes
4 oz. mushrooms
seasoning
1 beaten egg
few breadcrumbs
2 tablespoons grated cheese

1 Cook spaghetti in salted boiling water for 15–20 minutes.
2 Drain and cut into small lengths.
3 Heat the margarine; fry the finely chopped onion, peeled, sliced tomatoes and chopped mushrooms, until soft.
4 Mix with the spaghetti, seasoning, egg and enough breadcrumbs to make a sticky consistency.
5 Press into a greased medium-sized loaf tin and bake in the centre of a moderate oven (375°F.—Gas Mark 4) for 40 minutes.
6 Turn out and sprinkle with grated cheese.

**Variations:**

### Macaroni and mushroom loaf

Use the quick-cooking macaroni instead of spaghetti, cooking as directed on the packet. There is no need to chop the macaroni before mixing with the vegetables.

# Rice Dishes

## *Value of Rice*

Rice, like pasta, can be an excellent basis for meals without meat.
You can serve the cooked rice with cheese, tomato, anchovy sauce, etc., but this tends to make a slightly over-moist mixture. It is therefore better to cook a variety of ingredients in with the rice.

## Cheese rice

cooking time 20–25 minutes

**you will need for 4 servings:**

6 oz. long or medium grained rice
¾ pint water
½–1 teaspoon salt
pepper
approximately 8 oz. diced cheese or Cheddar
little chopped parsley
tomatoes and mushrooms for garnish

1 Put the rice with the cold water and salt into a saucepan, bring to the boil; put on the lid, lower the heat, and cook for approximately 20 minutes. With this method of cooking rice, all the liquid is absorbed and there is no fear of the rice being over-cooked.
2 Stir in the cheese, pepper and parsley.
3 Serve at once, garnished with fried tomatoes and mushrooms.

## Curried rice

cooking time few minutes

**you will need for 4 servings:**

2 oz. margarine
1–2 tablespoons curry powder
4–6 oz. cooked rice
few sultanas

1 Heat margarine.
2 Cook curry powder in this for a short time.
3 Gradually add cooked rice and sultanas.
4 Toss well together until hot.

**To serve Curried rice:**

This makes a complete meal when topped with a poached egg, scrambled egg, or with cheese. Although it is nicer hot, it can be part of a mixed salad.

## Vegetable risotto

cooking time approximately 30 minutes

**you will need for 4 servings:**

1 onion
3 tomatoes
4 oz. mushrooms
2 tablespoons oil
small green pepper
6 oz. rice
$\frac{3}{4}$ pint water
seasoning
grated Parmesan cheese

1 Chop the vegetables fairly finely.
2 Fry in the hot oil for about 10 minutes, until really very soft.
3 For the last 3 minutes put in the rice and blend thoroughly with the vegetable mixture.
4 Add the water, seasoning. Bring to the boil, lower the heat and cook for 15 minutes in a covered pan until all the liquid has been absorbed.
5 Serve topped with cheese.

## Mushroom risotto

cooking time 30 minutes

**you will need for 4 servings:**

3 tablespoons oil
2 small finely chopped onions
8 oz. long grain rice
2 chicken stock cubes
$1\frac{1}{2}$ pints water
4 oz. sliced mushrooms
2 oz. cooked peas
1 small chopped red pepper
1 small chopped green pepper
few black olives for garnish

1 Heat the oil; fry the onions and rice until golden brown, stirring frequently—about 10 minutes.
2 Add the crumbled chicken stock cubes and the water.
3 Bring to boil, stirring, then cover and simmer gently for about 10 minutes.
4 Add all the other ingredients and simmer for a further 10 minutes or until rice has absorbed all the liquid.
5 The risotto should be stirred occasionally whilst cooking.
6 Garnish with black olives.

## Potato rice croquettes

cooking time 35 minutes

**you will need for 4 servings:**

1 small onion
2 oz. butter or margarine
1 oz. flour
$\frac{1}{4}$ pint milk
1 teaspoon salt
1 teaspoon celery salt
2 teaspoons made mustard
pinch pepper
$\frac{1}{2}$ teaspoon lemon juice
8 oz. rice, cooked
8 oz. cooked potato
2 teaspoons minced parsley
1 egg
2 tablespoons water
few breadcrumbs for coating

1 Fry chopped onion in butter, until transparent.
2 Remove onion, add flour to butter and mix until smooth.
3 Add milk and cook until sauce thickens, stirring constantly.
4 Add salt, celery salt, mustard, pepper and lemon juice.
5 Mix sauce with onion, rice, potato and parsley.
6 Chill and then shape into balls.
7 Beat egg slightly and add water.
8 Roll the balls in the egg mixture and then coat with breadcrumbs.
9 Fry for about 3 minutes or until golden brown and drain on absorbent paper.

## Oriental rice

cooking time 20–25 minutes

**you will need for 4 servings:**

2 onions
8 oz. long grain rice
4 tablespoons oil
8 oz. mixed cooked vegetables
4 oz. prawns
1½ pints chicken stock or water and yeast extract or 1½ pints boiling water with 2 chicken stock cubes

1 Chop onions very finely and fry with the rice in the oil until just brown, stirring frequently to prevent the rice sticking.
2 Add the boiling water and yeast extract to the rice, cover and simmer gently for about 10 minutes.
3 Add the rest of the ingredients and simmer a further 10 minutes or until the rice has absorbed the liquid.

**Variation:**

Omit the cooked vegetables and prawns, and add 2 cinnamon sticks, 6 cloves and a pinch of turmeric. Continue as above.

## Rice and spinach savoury

cooking time 25 minutes

**you will need for 4 servings:**

2 oz. butter or margarine
1 onion
4 oz. rice
2 oz. grated cheese
1 lb. spinach, cooked or frozen
3 hard-boiled eggs
½ teaspoon salt
½ teaspoon celery salt
1 egg white
2 tablespoons mayonnaise (see page 73)

1 Melt butter in a large saucepan and fry onion until tender.
2 Cook rice in salted boiling water for 15 minutes until tender.
3 When cooked, add to onion together with the cheese, spinach, chopped eggs, salt and celery salt.
4 Cook over a low heat, stirring frequently, until cheese has melted and the mixture is hot all through.
5 Spoon mixture into baking dish.
6 Beat egg white until stiff but not dry.
7 Fold in mayonnaise and spread over rice mixture.
8 Put under the grill until topping is lightly browned for about 2 minutes.

## Rice and celery savoury

cooking time 25–30 minutes

**you will need for 4 servings:**

6 sticks celery
8 oz. rice
1 oz. blanched almonds
2 tablespoons chopped red or green peppers
1 medium can condensed vegetable soup
4 oz. grated cheese
½ teaspoon salt
pepper

1 Cut celery into ½-inch pieces and cook in boiling salted water until only slightly crisp.
2 Cook rice for 15 minutes in boiling salted water until tender.
3 Toss together drained celery and rice, chopped almonds and peppers.
4 Mix soup, cheese and salt together and cook until cheese has melted, stirring constantly.
5 Pour sauce over rice mixture and sprinkle with freshly ground pepper to taste and mix in thoroughly.
6 Serve at once.

**Variation:**

Follow the recipe as above, but replace the celery with prawns to make a rice and prawn savoury.

## Rice stuffed peppers

cooking time 45 minutes

**you will need for 4 servings:**

2 large green peppers
3 oz. rice
1½ oz. margarine
1 large onion
½ clove garlic
2 large tomatoes
4 sliced olives (optional)
seasoning

1 Cut the green peppers into halves across the middle.
2 Take out the cores and seeds.
3 Put peppers into boiling salted water and cook for 5 minutes only.
4 Cook rice in boiling salted water for 15 minutes until tender.
5 Drain peppers and rice well.
6 Heat the margarine and fry the chopped onion, garlic and sliced tomatoes.
7 When soft mix with the rice and olives, seasoning well.
8 Pile into the 4 halves of peppers and put into the centre of a moderate oven (375°F.—Gas Mark 4) and bake for 25 minutes.

# Vegetable Dishes

## *Value*

As explained in the beginning of this book, the foods that take the place of meat are the protein foods and therefore vegetables cannot be said to be a real substitute for meat.

They do, however, supply vitamins and add colour and eye-appeal to every dish. Combined imaginatively, they provide contrasting flavours as well as textures, and therefore interest and enjoyment.

Also, they form a splendid basis for sauces, etc., and provide the 'body' of a meal.

### Ratatouille

*(Illustrated in colour on the cover)*

cooking time 45 minutes

**you will need for 4 servings:**

2 large onions or about 8 very tiny onions
1 lb. tomatoes
1 medium marrow or 4–6 courgettes
4 small aubergines
little chopped parsley
1 red and 1 green pepper
2 tablespoons corn oil or 2 oz. fat
1–2 cloves garlic
seasoning
sprig thyme, 2 bay leaves

1. Chop the onions or halve the tiny onions.
2. Skin the tomatoes, then cut in half, sprinkle with salt and leave upturned to drain.
3. Peel the marrow, cut in large chunks or wash and thickly slice courgettes; remove stalks from the aubergines, cut in half, scoop out slightly and cut into chunks.
4. Seed, core and slice the peppers.
5. Heat the oil or fat in a strong pan and gently fry the onions and crushed garlic.
6. Add the aubergines, marrow or courgettes, tomatoes, peppers, thyme and bay leaves.
7. Season well and simmer slowly, with well-fitting lid on the pan, until the vegetables are tender.
8. Remove bay leaves, and serve, piping hot, sprinkled with parsley.

## *Vegetable casseroles*

A vegetable casserole is an ideal meal at any time of the year because it can be varied according to those vegetables that are in season.

It should, however, contain a reasonable proportion of the second-class protein vegetables to make it a satisfying meal.

Here is a basic recipe which can be varied according to the season.

cooking time approximately 1–1¼ hours

**you will need for 4 servings:**

8 small onions
4 good sized tomatoes
1 lb. French beans
8 medium-sized carrots
cauliflower
8 oz. peas or small packet frozen peas
2 oz. vegetarian fat or margarine
1 oz. flour
1 pint water
teaspoon yeast extract
seasoning
little chopped parsley

1. Peel the onions but leave them whole.
2. Skin and chop the tomatoes and make a purée.
3. Chop beans and carrots, break cauliflower into sprigs.
4. Heat the fat and toss the onions in this until a pale golden brown.
5. Lift out, then stir in the flour. Cook for 2 or 3 minutes then add water and yeast extract, bring to the boil and simmer until smooth.
6. Add the tomato purée, onions and carrots, simmer for approximately 30 minutes, then put in the beans.
7. For the last 15 minutes put in the cauliflower sprigs and peas and continue boiling.
8. Serve in a large casserole with creamed potatoes flavoured with plenty of grated cheese.

If preferred, this can be cooked in a moderate oven but, if you are adding vegetables like cauliflower and peas that need less cooking than the others, it is simpler to do it in a saucepan. It is, however, possible to plan the vegetables so that all of them need exactly the same time.

## Artichokes au gratin

cooking time approximately 50 minutes

**you will need for 4 servings:**

1–1½ lb. artichokes
little lemon juice
pinch salt
½–¾ pint cheese sauce (see page 63)
2 tablespoons grated cheese
2 tablespoons breadcrumbs
little margarine

1 Peel the artichokes and put them in cold water with a little lemon juice to keep them white.
2 Simmer gently for about 20 minutes in boiling salted water. They will not be quite tender, but take out and put into a pie dish.
3 Cover with cheese sauce, cheese, breadcrumbs and a little margarine.
4 Cook for approximately 30 minutes in the centre of a moderately hot oven (400°F.—Gas Mark 5), by which time they will be tender and very creamy in flavour.
5 Garnish with triangles of crisp toast or fried bread, as well as thin slices of tomato and mushrooms.

## Stuffed baby beetroot

cooking time 1¼–1½ hours

**you will need for 4 servings:**

*4 medium or 8 tiny uncooked beetroot
2 oz. fat for frying
2 large chopped onions
4 oz. grated cheese
breadcrumbs
seasoning

1 Allow 1 or 2 beetroots per person.
2 Cook, peel and trim to a good shape.
3 Cut slice off top and scoop out centre—these pieces are diced and used in salads.
4 Fill centre of beetroots with fried onion and cheese and breadcrumbs.
5 Reheat gently.
*Cooked beetroots could be used.

## Stuffed cabbage No. 1

cooking time 1 hour 15 minutes

**you will need for 4 servings:**

8 large cabbage leaves
2 oz. rice
1 large skinned and chopped tomato
3 oz. grated cheese
1 or 2 hard-boiled eggs
seasoning to taste
½ pint brown sauce (see page 64)

1 Wash cabbage leaves well and put into boiling salted water, until soft and easy to roll.
2 Drain well.
3 Cook the rice for 15 minutes in boiling salted water until tender.
4 Blend rice with the tomato, cheese and chopped hard-boiled eggs and season.
5 Put spoonfuls of the mixture into each cabbage leaf, roll firmly and secure with cotton.
6 Put into a casserole, cover with brown sauce.
7 Cover with a lid or foil and cook for about 1 hour in a very moderate oven (350°F.—Gas Mark 3).

**Variation:**
Use tomato sauce (see page 65) instead of brown sauce.

## Stuffed cabbage No. 2

cooking time 35 minutes

**you will need for 4 servings:**

8 outer cabbage leaves
1 can baked beans
2 eggs
1 oz. butter
½ teaspoon mixed herbs
2 oz. grated cheese
salt and pepper
tomato sauce (see page 65)

1 Select good-sized cabbage leaves. Cook in boiling salted water for 5 minutes to soften. Drain and cool.
2 Mix the beans, eggs, cheese, butter, herbs and seasoning and stuff the cabbage leaves, rolling them up neatly, fastening with cotton.
3 Put in casserole, pour over tomato sauce and bake, covered, for 35 minutes in moderate oven (375°F.—Gas Mark 4).

## Carrot loaf

cooking time 1 hour 20 minutes

**you will need for 4 servings:**

1 lb. cooked carrots
½ pint white sauce (see page 63)
good pinch salt, pepper, mixed spice
1 oz. breadcrumbs
2 hard-boiled eggs
1–2 oz. margarine or butter
crisp breadcrumbs

1 Drain the carrots well and chop into small pieces or sieve. It is better to cook them whole and cut afterwards—otherwise they tend to be too wet.
2 Mix carrots with the sauce, seasoning, breadcrumbs and 1 chopped egg.
3 Put the mixture into a greased loaf tin—coated with crumbs. Use remaining margarine to put in small knobs on top of the loaf.

4 Bake in the middle of a very moderate oven (350°F.—Gas Mark 3) for 1 hour.
5 Turn out and decorate with remaining chopped egg. Serve with green peas and creamed potatoes.

**Variations:**

### Artichoke loaf
Substitute globe artichokes for carrots.

### Cheese and vegetable loaf
Cheese sauce (see page 63) for white sauce.

### Potato loaf
Firm cooked potatoes for carrots.

### Mixed vegetable loaf
Carrots, turnip, parsnip, swede instead of all carrots.

### Tomato and vegetable loaf
Tomato sauce (see page 65) for white sauce.

## Stuffed cauliflower

cooking time 25 minutes

**you will need for 4 servings:**

- 1 medium sized cauliflower
- 1–3 chopped hard-boiled eggs
- 1 tablespoon chopped gherkin or cucumber
- ¼ pint thick tomato sauce (see page 65)
- 1 tablespoon grated cheese
- few capers

1 Cook the cauliflower whole.
2 When soft, scoop out centre.
3 Mix with all the other ingredients, except cheese.
4 Pile into the centre of the cauliflower.
5 Sprinkle with cheese.
6 Brown under grill or in the oven. Decorate with capers and serve piping hot.

**Variations:**

### Prawn stuffing
3 oz. chopped prawns instead of cheese, and white (see page 63) instead of tomato sauce.

### Cheese stuffing
Cheese (see page 63) instead of tomato sauce.

## Cauliflower and eggs au gratin

cooking time 45 minutes

**you will need for 4 servings:**

- 1 medium sized cauliflower
- 2 hard-boiled eggs
- 2 oz. margarine
- 1 oz. flour
- ¼ pint milk
- vegetable stock
- seasoning
- 3 tablespoons grated cheese
- 2 tablespoons crisp breadcrumbs

1 Divide the cauliflower into neat pieces. Cook until just tender in boiling salted water. Keep ¼ pint of the vegetable water, and drain the cauliflower well.
2 Put the cauliflower at the bottom of a greased pie dish, cover with sliced eggs.
3 Heat 1 oz. margarine in a good-sized saucepan, stir in the flour, and cook gently for a few minutes.
4 Remove the pan from the heat, and gradually stir in milk and vegetable stock. Return to heat and bring to the boil, stirring all the time.
5 Cook until thickened, then season well, and add half the cheese. Pour over the cauliflower, sprinkle with breadcrumbs, rest of the cheese and margarine.
6 Put into a moderately hot oven (425°F.—Gas Mark 6) and bake for 25 minutes.

## Cauliflower and tomato fritters

cooking time 20 minutes

**you will need for 4 servings:**

- 4 tomatoes
- 1 small cauliflower
- good pinch salt
- 4 oz. flour
- 1 egg
- fat or oil for frying
- cayenne pepper

1 Rub tomatoes through sieve—measure and if necessary add little water to make ¼ pint.
2 Divide the cauliflower into neat sprigs—try to keep them uniform in size. Cook in boiling salted water until just soft, but unbroken. Drain well.
3 Sieve the flour and salt together.
4 Add the well-beaten egg and gradually beat in the tomato purée.
5 Put the pieces of cauliflower into this batter and, when well coated, drop in boiling fat and cook until crisp and brown.
6 Dust with cayenne pepper and serve at once.

**Variations:**

### Cheese cauliflower
Substitute ⅜ pint milk and 2 oz. grated cheese for tomato purée.

### Creamy cauliflower
⅜ pint milk for tomato purée.

## Chicory cargoes

cooking time 45–55 minutes

**you will need for 4 servings:**

4 large chicory heads
1 medium onion
$1\frac{1}{2}$ oz. butter
3 oz. chopped mushrooms
4 oz. grated cheese
3 oz. white breadcrumbs
little milk
lemon juice
parsley
salt

1 Remove root ends from the chicory, discarding any tough outer leaves.
2 Wipe the chicory heads and split them in half lengthways.
3 Hollow out, removing the smallest inner leaves to leave space for the filling.
4 Finely chop the onion, fry gently in 1 oz. butter until soft.
5 Add the mushrooms and fry for a further 3 minutes.
6 Chop the inner chicory leaves and mix with the cheese, breadcrumbs and vegetables, moistening well with milk.
7 Fill the cases, dot with butter and place in a greased fireproof dish.
8 Cover with kitchen foil and bake for 30–45 minutes at 325°F.—Gas Mark 3.
9 Sprinkle with a little lemon juice, salt and parsley and serve with melted butter.

## Glazed mushrooms

cooking time 15–20 minutes

**you will need for 4 servings:**

1 lb. mushrooms
$\frac{1}{8}$ pint water
1 oz. butter
1 oz. flour
$\frac{1}{2}$ pint milk
1 egg yolk
3 oz. grated cheese
juice 1 lemon
1 oz. fresh breadcrumbs

1 Wash and halve mushrooms and simmer in a little water for 5 minutes.
2 Melt butter, add flour and cook gently for 1 minute.
3 Beat in milk and cook until thickened.
4 Remove from heat and beat in yolk, cheese and lemon juice.
5 Place mushrooms in a dish.
6 Pour over sauce.
7 Sprinkle with breadcrumbs and brown under a hot grill.

## Farmhouse supper dish

cooking time 40 minutes

**you will need for 4 servings:**

1 medium cauliflower
4 carrots
2–3 hard-boiled eggs
1 packet leek soup powder
1 pint water
3 slices bread

1 Cook the cauliflower and carrots, then slice carrots and break the cauliflower into sprigs.
2 Arrange with the carrots and sliced eggs in layers in a greased casserole.
3 Make up leek soup with 1 pint water and bring to the boil.
4 Pour over ingredients in the casserole.
5 Toast bread, cut into small cubes and sprinkle around edge of casserole.
6 Cook for 20 minutes in a moderately hot oven (400°F.—Gas Mark 5).

## Stuffed marrow

cooking time 1 hour 5 minutes

**you will need for 4 servings:**

1 marrow
1 oz. butter or margarine
2 onions
3 carrots
2 tomatoes
4 oz. sliced mushrooms
4 oz. grated cheese
seasoning
2 oz. brown breadcrumbs

1 Skin marrow, cut off top and remove pips.
2 Melt butter and fry chopped onion, carrots and tomatoes for 5 minutes.
3 Add mushrooms, half the cheese and seasoning.
4 Remove from heat and stir in breadcrumbs.
5 Place half the vegetable and cheese mixture in the scooped-out marrow.
6 Cover with remaining cheese and vegetable mixture, sprinkle over rest of grated cheese.
7 Replace marrow top and place in dish and cover with foil.
8 Bake in a moderate oven (375°F.—Gas Mark 4) for approximately 1 hour.

## Onion grill

cooking time 20–25 minutes

**you will need for 4 servings:**

1 lb. sliced onions
2 oz. butter
1 oz. flour
$\frac{1}{2}$ pint milk
4 oz. grated Cheddar cheese
2 level tablespoons brown breadcrumbs

Cook onions gently in butter with the lid on the pan.
When soft but not coloured, stir in the flour.
Add milk and stir over heat until the sauce is creamy.
Pour into a buttered dish and cover with cheese and breadcrumbs.
Brown under the grill.

## Savoury stuffed onions

cooking time 1¼ hours

**you will need for 4 servings:**

- 4 medium-sized onions
- seasoning
- 1 teaspoon sage
- 1 fresh egg
- 2 oz. breadcrumbs
- little margarine
- ½ pint cheese sauce (see page 63)
- parsley for garnish

Put the onions into salted water and boil steadily for 30 minutes. By this time they will not be completely cooked but it should be possible to remove the centre core. Keep stock.
Chop the onion cores finely, add remaining ingredients and pile this stuffing back into the centres.
Put the onions into a greased casserole. Pour over ⅓ pint of onion stock and put a small piece of margarine on each onion.
Bake for 45 minutes, covered, in moderately hot oven (400°F.—Gas Mark 5).
Serve with cheese sauce. Garnish with parsley.

**Variations:**

### Vegetable stuffed onions

Stuff with about 6 oz. chopped cooked mixed vegetables blended with 2 eggs and mixed herbs.

### Cheese stuffed onions

Mix onion cores with approximately 4 oz. grated cheese and 2 oz. breadcrumbs. Blend with 1 oz. margarine or butter and just a little milk. Omit egg.

### Rice stuffed onions

Substitute 2–3 oz. cooked rice for breadcrumbs.

### Tomato stuffed onions

Blend chopped onion cores with 2–3 skinned chopped tomatoes and 3 chopped hard-boiled eggs. Season well. Add about 1 oz. breadcrumbs if desired.

## Onion potato soufflé

cooking time 50 minutes

**you will need for 4 servings:**

- 1 lb. potatoes
- 1 large chopped onion
- 2 oz. butter or margarine
- 1 teaspoon salt
- 1 tablespoon finely chopped parsley
- ⅛ pint hot milk
- 4 eggs

1 Cook and mash potatoes.
2 Fry onion in margarine, then add to potato, with milk, parsley and salt.
3 Stir in egg yolks and then add the stiffly beaten whites.
4 Pour into a soufflé dish and bake for approximately 25–30 minutes in the centre of a moderately hot oven (400°F.—Gas Mark 5).

## Onion rice soufflé

cooking time approximately 1 hour

**you will need for 4 servings:**

- 2 large onions
- 3 oz. rice
- ½ pint thick white sauce (see page 63)
- 4 eggs
- ¼ teaspoon nutmeg
- 2 tablespoons chopped parsley
- ¼ teaspoon paprika
- ½ teaspoon basil or powdered sage

1 Boil onions until tender.
2 Cook rice in slightly salted water until tender.
3 Drain onions and rice thoroughly; chop onions finely.
4 Gradually add the sauce to the slightly beaten egg yolks and nutmeg.
5 Blend in rice, onions, parsley and seasonings.
6 Beat egg whites until stiff and fold into mixture.
7 Pour into an ungreased 2-pint casserole or soufflé dish and bake in centre of a very moderate oven (350°F.—Gas Mark 3) for 45 minutes.
8 Serve at once.

## Stuffed peppers

cooking time 30 minutes

**you will need for 4 servings:**

4 medium sized green or red peppers (capsicums)
1 good tablespoon oil or 1½ oz. margarine
1 large onion
2 oz. mushrooms
3 oz. cooked rice
seasoning

1 Cut the peppers into halves crossways. Take out the centres and seeds.
2 Put into boiling salted water and cook for 5 minutes. Drain well.
3 Heat oil or margarine, fry the chopped onion, sliced mushrooms and season. When soft, mix with the rice.
4 Pile into halved peppers.
5 Put into the middle of a moderate oven (375°F.—Gas Mark 4) and bake for 25 minutes.
Serve with a cheese sauce (see page 63).

**Variation:**

### Cheese stuffed peppers

Add 3 oz. grated cheese to rice and onion with little chopped parsley. Omit mushrooms.

### Prawn stuffed peppers

Follow the recipe as above, but add prawns dipped in lemon juice to the rice and onion.

## Jacket potatoes

cooking time 45 minutes

**you will need for 4 servings:**

1 Choose 4 evenly sized potatoes and scrub scrupulously clean.
2 Dry and rub well with oiled tissue paper.
3 Bake in moderately hot oven (400°F.—Gas Mark 5) for 45 minutes.
4 Before serving, slightly break to let out steam and make floury.

**Note:**

Overcooked jacket potatoes means potato pulp all over the oven. Careful timing prevents this, so does pricking lightly all over with a fork.
The time, i.e. 45 minutes, is for only medium-sized potatoes. Really large potatoes will take up to 1¼–1½ hours at the same temperature.

## Potato nests

cooking time from 10–15 minutes

**you will need for 4 servings:**

4 baked potatoes
butter or margarine
seasoning
4 eggs
little cream or grated cheese

1 Remove the potato pulp, mash with margarine or butter and seasoning.
2 Pile back into the potato cases, leaving a large well in the centre.
3 Break an egg into each, add a little seasoning and a small amount of cream or a sprinkling of grated cheese.
4 Return to the oven (400°F.–Gas Mark 5) for 10–15 minutes to set the eggs.

**Variation:**

Follow the recipe as above but omit the eggs and add prawns dipped in lemon juice to the mashed potato. Pile back into the potato cases and serve immediately.

## Cheese potatoes

cooking time from 10–15 minutes

**you will need for 4 servings:**

4 large potatoes
butter or margarine
seasoning
grated cheese

1 Mix the pulp of the cooked jacket potatoes with a knob of margarine or butter, seasoning and grated cheese.
2 Pile or pipe back into the potato cases and warm through.
Do not overcook or the cheese will become very stringy.

**Variation:**

For slimmers, follow the recipe as above but substitute cottage cheese.

## Potato and parsnip pie

cooking time about 35–45 minutes

**you will need for 4 servings:**

1½ lb. baked potatoes
4 oz. grated cheese
seasoning
1 egg
**For filling:**
2 lb. parsnips
2 tablespoons vinegar
4–6 oz. grated cheese
seasoning
1 egg
1 level teaspoon mustard

1 Boil, drain and mash or sieve potatoes.
2 Beat cheese into hot potato.

3 Stir in seasoning and beaten egg.
4 Cover base of greased oven-proof dish with potato.
5 Boil parsnips in water and vinegar.
6 Strain and dice finely.
7 Add cheese and mix well.
8 Stir in seasoning, beaten egg and mustard.
9 Pile on to potato and bake in a moderately hot oven (400°F.—Gas Mark 5) for 20–25 minutes until golden brown.
10 Serve hot.

**Variation:**

The mixture can be topped with breadcrumbs and extra grated cheese to give a crunchy topping.

## Potatoes au gratin

cooking time 35–40 minutes

**you will need for 4 servings:**

| | |
|---|---|
| 1 lb. peeled potatoes | vegetable stock |
| 2 oz. butter or margarine | 6 oz. Cheddar cheese |
| 2 oz. flour | seasoning |
| ¼ pint milk | paprika pepper |

1 Dice and cook peeled potatoes until just tender, strain, keep ¼ pint vegetable stock.
2 Melt butter, stir in the flour. When well blended, add milk and stock, and cook, stirring constantly, until mixture has thickened and become smooth.
3 Add 5 oz. cheese and stir over low heat until the cheese is melted, do not overcook. Remove from heat, season.
4 Add the potatoes.
5 Turn the mixture into a greased pie dish or shallow casserole and top with the remainder of the cheese and a generous sprinkling of paprika.
6 Bake in a moderately hot oven (400°F.—Gas Mark 5) for about 20 minutes or until bubbly and brown, or put for short time under hot grill. A layer of breadcrumbs can be put on top as well as cheese.

**Variations:**

## Asparagus au gratin

Arrange cooked or canned tips in a shallow dish with tips to centre.

## Beans au gratin

Any cooked beans—green, haricot or butter—instead of potatoes.

## Cabbage au gratin

Shred cabbage coarsely and cook quickly until only just tender. Do not mix with sauce but arrange sauce, etc. over cabbage. A layer of sliced hard-boiled egg can be put *over* cabbage. Or use Brussels sprouts instead of cabbage. Chopped fried onion mixed with cabbage, gives extra flavour.

## Carrots au gratin

Substitute whole cooked young carrots or diced older carrots for potatoes, using more milk and less stock.

## Cauliflower au gratin

Cut cauliflower into sprigs before cooking. Arrange in shallow dish with heads upmost before coating with cheese, etc.

## Celery au gratin

Dice and cook celery until tender. All celery stock gives good flavour to the sauce, or use ½ milk and ½ celery stock.

## Chicory au gratin

Cook the white head until just tender—use rather less stock and more milk than for potatoes.

## Leeks au gratin

Keep leeks whole if small—split into halves if large.

## Marrow au gratin

Steam rather than boil, diced or rings of marrow so it does not become 'watery'. Arrange in hot dish, coat with sauce and brown under grill.

## Onions au gratin

Serve whole onions if small—if large, cut into thick slices before cooking.

## Vegetables au gratin

Mixed vegetables can be served in the same way.

## Potato casserole

cooking time about 35 minutes

**you will need for 4 servings:**

- 5 medium-sized potatoes
- 2 oz. margarine
- 1 medium-sized chopped onion
- 2 oz. crisp breadcrumbs
- 4 oz. grated cheese
- 2 well-beaten eggs
- ⅜ pint milk
- 1 teaspoon salt
- dash pepper

1. Cook potatoes in boiling water until tender, drain and peel. When cool, cut in thin slices.
2. Melt the margarine, add the onion and cook until tender but not brown.
3. Put the potatoes in a 1-quart casserole and sprinkle over onion, breadcrumbs and cheese.
4. Combine eggs, milk, salt and pepper; pour mixture over the potatoes. Top with additional grated cheese, if desired.
5. Bake in a moderate oven (350°F.—Gas Mark 3) for 20 minutes.

## Potato kuku

cooking time 1¼ hours

**you will need for 4 servings:**

- 1 lb. cooked potatoes
- little milk
- 1 tablespoon grated onion
- ½ teaspoon salt
- ¼ teaspoon pepper
- ¼ teaspoon chopped parsley
- 6 eggs
- 2 oz. melted butter or margarine

1. Mash potatoes with milk. Stir in onion, salt, pepper and parsley.
2. Whisk eggs until thick and light.
3. Beat in potato mixture to combine well.
4. Pour butter into 4-pint casserole and add potato and egg mixture.
5. Bake for 45–50 minutes in very moderate oven (350°F.—Gas Mark 3) until firm.

## Baked soufflé potatoes

cooking time 15 minutes

**you will need for 4 servings:**

- 4 large baked potatoes
- 2 egg yolks
- seasoning
- 1 tablespoon cream or top of milk
- 2 stiffly beaten egg whites

1. Cut off tops of potatoes, scoop out pulp and sieve or mash.
2. Add the yolks of eggs, cream or top of milk, seasoning and the stiffiy beaten egg whites.
3. Pile back into the potato cases and cook in moderate oven (375°F.—Gas Mark 4) for 15 minutes until just pale golden brown.

**Variations:**

### Baked cheese soufflé potatoes

Add 2–3 oz. grated cheese to potato pulp.

### Baked tomato soufflé potatoes

Add sieved or mashed pulp of 2–3 tomatoes to potato pulp.

## Spinach stuffed tomatoes

cooking time 20 minutes

**you will need for 4 servings:**

- 4 large tomatoes
- 1 oz. margarine
- 1 teaspoon finely chopped onion
- 2 heaped tablespoons cooked, chopped spinach
- 1 tablespoon top of milk
- seasoning
- 4 slices Cheddar cheese

1. Cut a slice from the top of each tomato and scoop out the centre.
2. Cut finely.
3. Heat margarine and fry the onion until soft.
4. Mix with the spinach, top of the milk, seasoning and tomato pulp.
5. Put mixture into tomato cases and lay slices of cheese, cut to the size of the tomatoes, on top.
6. Replace the 'lids' of the tomatoes and cook in the centre of a moderate oven (375°F.—Gas Mark 4) for 10 minutes.

## Spinach soufflé

cooking time approximately 30–35 minutes

**you will need for 4 servings:**

- 1 oz. butter
- 1 oz. flour
- ½ pint smooth spinach purée
- 2 tablespoons cream
- seasoning
- 3 egg yolks
- 1 oz. Parmesan cheese (optional)
- 4 egg whites

1. Heat the butter.
2. Stir in the flour.
3. Gradually add spinach purée.
4. Bring to boil, cook until thickened and smooth.

5 Add cream, cheese (if being used), seasoning, yolks, and last the stiffly beaten egg whites.
6 Pour into soufflé dish.
7 Bake for approximately 30 to 35 minutes in the centre of a moderate oven (375°F.—Gas Mark 4).

### Tomato and mushroom towers

cooking time 20–25 minutes

**you will need for 4 servings:**

8 tomatoes
2 onions
1 oz. butter
seasoning
5 oz. grated Cheddar cheese
8 good size button mushrooms
extra butter

1 Slice off tomato tops and remove pulp.
2 Chop onion and lightly fry in melted butter.
3 Season well and mix cheese to a paste with the tomato pulp.
4 Stalk the mushrooms, chop and mix them with the cheese paste, setting aside the whole mushroom caps.
5 Place the tomatoes in a fireproof dish, putting cooked onions inside and spreading the cheese mixture on the undersides of the mushrooms.
6 Sit a mushroom on top of each tomato and cover with tomato lids.
7 Brush over with butter and bake at 425–450°F.—Gas Mark 6–7 for about 15 minutes.

### Tomato meringues

cooking time 10 minutes

**you will need for 4 servings:**

4 large tomatoes
2 eggs
seasoning
2 oz. grated Cheddar cheese
2 tablespoons breadcrumbs

1 Slice tops from tomatoes and scoop out pulp.
2 Cut this finely.
3 Whisk the egg yolks, add tomato pulp, cheese and breadcrumbs.
4 Season well and pile into tomato cases.
5 Whip the egg whites until very stiff, adding a pinch of salt and pepper.
6 Pile on top of the tomato cases.
7 Put into the centre of a moderate oven (375°F.—Gas Mark 4) for 10 minutes.

### Vegetable curry

cooking time 1 hour 20 minutes

Recipe as for curried eggs (see page 32) adding 1 lb. mixed vegetables (beans, carrots, diced turnips—very few as they have a strong flavour) with the other ingredients.
Simmer for about 35 minutes and serve in a border of boiled rice.

# Pastries

Pastry not only makes a dish more substantial, but also it can turn an otherwise light dish into one suitable for a main meal.
Even if the recipe does not call for pastry, a cheese pastry such as the one on this page, can be baked, cut in fingers, and served with a soup or with a vegetable dish, so that the cheese and egg will be adding to the food value.
There is an unusual variation of short crust pastry in this chapter, i.e. Devilled short crust. It can be used with any savoury recipe instead of ordinary short crust, as it gives a very distinctive flavour.

### Cheese pastry

cooking time 30 minutes

**you will need for 4 servings:**

8 oz. flour
1 level teaspoon dry mustard
4 oz. vegetable fat or margarine
2–3 oz. finely grated Cheddar cheese
cold water to mix

1 Sieve flour and mustard.
2 Rub in fat until mixture resembles fine breadcrumbs.
3 Add cheese.
4 Mix to a dry dough with water.
5 Bake in a hot oven (425°F.—Gas Mark 7).

## Rich cheese pastry

cooking time — as individual recipe

**you will need for 2 oz. pastry:**

1½ oz. margarine or butter
2 oz. flour
1½ oz. finely grated cheese
seasoning
beaten egg yolk, or milk to mix

1 Rub the margarine or butter into the flour until it has the consistency of breadcrumbs.
2 Add the cheese and plenty of seasoning.
3 Make into a firm dough with egg yolk or milk.
4 Always bake cheese pastry in a really hot oven (450°F.—Gas Mark 7) and cool for a few minutes before removing from baking tin, as it is very brittle.

## Flaky pastry

cooking time — as individual recipe

**you will need for 4 servings:**

8 oz. plain flour
pinch salt
5–6 oz. fat
water to mix

1 Sieve flour with salt.
2 Divide fat into 3 portions.
3 Rub 1 portion into flour in usual way and mix to a rolling consistency with cold water.
4 Roll out to oblong shape.
5 Take the second portion of fat, divide it into small pieces and lay them on surface of two-thirds of the dough. Leave remaining third without fat.
6 Take its corners and fold back over second third so that the dough looks like an envelope with its flap open.
7 Fold over top end of pastry, so closing the 'envelope'.
8 Turn pastry at right angles, seal open ends of pastry and 'rib' it. This means depressing it with the rolling pin at intervals, so giving a corrugated effect and equalising the pressure of air. This makes certain the pastry will rise evenly.
9 Repeat the process again using the remaining fat and turning pastry in same way.
10 Roll out pastry once more, but should it begin to feel very soft and sticky put into a cold place for 30 minutes to become firm before again rolling out.
11 Fold pastry as before, turn it, seal edges and 'rib' it. Altogether the pastry should have 3 foldings and 3 rollings.
12 Stand in a cold place for a little while before baking since the contrast between the cold and the heat of the oven makes the pastry rise better.
13 Baking times and temperatures are given in the individual recipes, but as a general rule bake in a very hot oven (475°F.—Gas Mark 8) for first 15 minutes, after this lower the Gas Mark to 5 or 6, or turn an electric oven off, to finish cooking for remaining time at a lower temperature.

## Flan pastry

cooking time — as individual recipe

**you will need for 4 servings:**

4 oz. vegetarian fat
little sugar
1 egg yolk
8 oz. flour (either white or wholemeal)
little water

1 Cream fat thoroughly and add a little sugar.
2 Work in the flour.
3 Mix to a firm dough with the yolk and water.
4 Bake in a hot oven (425°F.—Gas Mark 7).

**Variation:**

### Rich flan pastry

Method as above using 5 oz. fat to 8 oz. flour. Handle with care when rolling out and kneading and bake in a moderately hot oven.

## Puff pastry

cooking time — as individual recipe

**you will need:**

8 oz. flour
good pinch salt
cold water to mix
few drops lemon juice
7–8 oz. fat.

1 Sieve flour and salt together.
2 Mix to rolling consistency with cold water and lemon juice.

3 Roll to oblong shape.
4 Make fat into neat block and place in centre of pastry and fold over it first the bottom section of pastry and then the top section, so that fat is completely covered.
5 Turn the dough at right angles, seal edges and 'rib' carefully (see flaky pastry, opposite) and roll out.
6 Fold dough into envelopes, turn it, seal edges, 'rib' and roll again.
7 Repeat 5 times, so making 7 rollings and 7 foldings in all.
8 Put pastry to rest in cold place once or twice between rollings to prevent it becoming sticky and soft. Always put to rest before rolling for the last time and before baking.
9 Bake for the first 10–15 minutes at 475–500°F.—Gas Mark 8–9, then lower to Gas Mark 5–6 or turn electric oven right out or re-set to 400°F. to finish cooking at lower temperature.
10 Well made puff pastry should rise to 4 or 5 times its original thickness.

## Suet crust pastry

cooking time as individual recipe

**you will need for 4 servings:**

8 oz. self-raising flour (with plain flour 2 level teaspoons baking powder)
pinch salt
2–4 oz. finely shredded suet
water to mix

1 Sieve flour, salt and baking powder together.
2 Add suet and mix to a rolling consistency with cold water.
3 Roll out thinly, as this pastry rises.
4 Line a pudding basin with the dough, leaving some over for the cover.
5 Put in the filling and put on the pastry cover.
6 Put greased greaseproof paper on cover and wrap in a pudding cloth.
7 Steam or boil rapidly for 2–3 hours, depending on filling.
Make sure the water is boiling rapidly when the pudding goes in and, when necessary, replenish, but always with boiling water.

## Short crust pastry

cooking time as individual recipe

**you will need for 4 servings:**

8 oz. flour (either white or wholemeal)
pinch salt
4 oz. vegetarian fat, margarine or fat and margarine mixed
water to mix

1 Sieve flour and salt together.
2 Rub in the fat until the consistency of fine breadcrumbs.
3 Mix to a firm dough with the water, being careful not to over-handle.
4 Roll out and use as required.

**Note:**

Wholemeal flour uses more water than ordinary flour.

## Devilled short crust

cooking time as individual recipe

**you will need for 4 servings:**

6 oz. flour
¼ level teaspoon salt
1 level teaspoon paprika
1 level teaspoon dry mustard
pinch white pepper
4 oz. butter
1 oz. grated Cheddar cheese
1 egg yolk
1 tablespoon water

1 Sift flour with salt, paprika, mustard and white pepper.
2 Rub in butter, add cheese and mix to a dry dough with egg yolk beaten with the water.
3 Use in place of short crust pastry in various dishes.

## Cheese shortbread

cooking time 25 minutes

**you will need for 4 servings:**

4 oz. butter or margarine
4 oz. sharp cheese, coarsely grated
4 oz. flour
Worcestershire sauce
paprika, cayenne or any other seasoning desired
walnut halves to garnish

1 Combine all ingredients, except walnuts, working with the hands for a good blend.
2 Form into balls.
3 Place balls on an ungreased baking sheet and flatten with a fork.
4 Put half a walnut on top of each and bake in a moderate oven (375°F.—Gas Mark 4) for 25 minutes.

# Pastry Dishes

### *Making flans and pies*

When making a flan the easiest utensil to use is a flan ring, which is placed on a baking sheet. If you turn the sheet upside down in the oven, before putting the ring in place, it is far easier to remove the flan when cooked. Otherwise use an ordinary sandwich tin, or where there is a fairly substantial filling, a pie dish, which is lined with the pastry, or a pie plate.

In some of the recipes you are told to bake the flan 'blind'. This means baking it without a filling. To keep the pastry a good shape, put a sheet of greased greaseproof paper and crusts of bread or beans on to the pastry. This holds the base flat and, at the same time, keeps the shape.

Take the paper and beans or bread out after about 20 minutes, then return flan to the oven for a further 5–10 minutes, to make sure the pastry is brown.

When using a flan ring, slip this away at the same time as the paper, etc. is removed, so the outside becomes crisp.

With a sandwich tin or pie plate, however, it is unwise to take the paper and beans away before the pastry is thoroughly cooked, as it can so easily break.

It is traditional that a savoury flan is baked in a plain rather than a fluted ring, but this, of course, is really a matter of personal taste.

### *To bake a pie*

To have a good shape to the pie, line the rim of the pie dish with a narrow strip of pastry before putting on the cover. Flute or shape the edges neatly before baking.

### *Use the right pastry*

While the individual recipes suggest the pastry, you can make changes by using flan pastry instead of short crust, or using flaky or puff in the pies. These richer pastries, which rise a great deal, are less satisfactory in flans because they do not keep such a good shape. If using them for the top of a pie, start with a hotter oven than for short crust, as this gives the pastry a chance to rise.

## Aubergine and tomato flan

cooking time 35 minutes

**you will need for 4 servings:**

- 4 oz. short crust pastry (see page 55)
- 1 small aubergine
- 3 tomatoes
- 1 oz. margarine
- 2 eggs
- salt and pepper

1. Roll out pastry on a lightly floured board and line an 8-inch flan ring or sandwich tin.
2. Peel aubergine, cut into 4 lengthwise, then slice.
3. Peel tomatoes and cut two into eighths.
4. Cook aubergine and tomato gently in margarine for 5–10 minutes, until tender.
5. Beat eggs lightly with seasoning.
6. Allow aubergine and tomato to cool slightly, add to the eggs and pour into the flan.
7. Bake in a moderately hot oven (400°F.—Gas Mark 5), on the second shelf from the top, for 30–35 minutes.
8. Cut remaining tomato into thin slices and place on flan 5 minutes before end of cooking.
9. Serve hot or cold.

## Béchamel flan

cooking time 40–45 minutes

**you will need for 4 servings:**

6 oz. flan or short crust pastry (see page 55)

**For filling:**

¾ pint Béchamel sauce (see page 63)
3 eggs
¼ pint thick cream
6 oz. grated Cheddar cheese
salt and pepper
pinch nutmeg

1. Line an 8-inch flan ring with pastry and place on a hot baking sheet.
2. Make Béchamel sauce and allow to cool.
3. Add beaten eggs gradually.
4. Stir in cream, cheese, seasoning and nutmeg thoroughly.
5. Pour filling into flan.
6. Bake towards bottom of moderately hot oven (400°F —Gas Mark 5) for 40–45 minutes, removing flan ring after 35 minutes to allow pastry to cook thoroughly.
7. Serve hot or cold.

## Cheese flan

cooking time 30–40 minutes

**you will need for 4 servings:**

**For pastry:**

4 oz. plain flour
2 oz. self-raising flour
or
6 oz. plain flour
½ teaspoon baking powder
½ teaspoon salt
pinch cayenne pepper
1½ oz. butter
3 oz. grated cheese
3 tablespoons cold water
squeeze lemon juice

**For filling:**

3 eggs
½ pint milk
1 dessertspoon cornflour
salt and cayenne
½ teaspoon grated nutmeg
1 oz. butter

1. Sieve flours, salt and cayenne.
2. Cut in the butter.
3. Add cheese and mix to form dough with water and lemon juice.
4. Roll out thinly and line a shallow 8-inch square or round tin.
5. Beat eggs, milk, cornflour and seasoning well together.
6. Pour into flan case.
7. Sprinkle with nutmeg and dot with butter.
8. Bake in centre of moderately hot oven (400°F. —Gas Mark 5) for approximately 30–40 minutes until filling is set.

## Cheese and vegetable flan

cooking time 40–45 minutes

**you will need for 6 to 7 servings:**

6 oz. short crust pastry (see page 55)
2 eggs
⅜ pint warm milk
seasoning
selection cooked vegetables—diced young carrots, turnips, beans, peas, beetroot, tomato (raw), cucumber (raw)
4 oz. grated cheese

1. Line a deep flan ring or oblong tin with the short crust pastry.
2. Bake 'blind' for 10–15 minutes in a hot oven (425–450°F.—Gas Mark 6–7).
3. Beat eggs, add milk and seasoning.
4. Arrange vegetables in the flan.
5. Stir cheese into mixture and pour over the vegetables.
6. Bake for about 30 minutes in a moderate oven (375°F.—Gas Mark 4) until the filling is quite firm.
7. Serve hot or cold.

**Variation:**

For a plain vegetable flan, omit the grated cheese and add some chopped parsley.

## Creamed corn flan

cooking time 25–30 minutes

**you will need for 4 servings:**

6 oz. short crust pastry (see page 55)
½ oz. butter or margarine
½ oz. cornflour
milk if necessary
large can creamed corn
2 eggs
seasoning
little grated Parmesan cheese

1. Roll out pastry and line a 7-inch flan ring or tin and bake 'blind' for 25–30 minutes until golden brown and crisp.
2. Melt the butter or margarine in a saucepan.
3. Add cornflour and cook for a few minutes to form a roux.
4. Add the corn, made up to ½ pint with milk if necessary, and cook, stirring, for a further 1 minute.
5. Remove from the heat and add the beaten yolks and seasoning to taste.
6. Fold in the stiffly beaten whites.
7. Turn into the flan case and sprinkle with grated cheese.
8. Bake in a moderately hot oven (400°F.—Gas Mark 5) for 20–25 minutes.

## Farmer's flan

cooking time 35–40 minutes

**you will need for 4 servings:**

6 oz. shortcrust pastry or devilled short crust (see page 55)
2 tomatoes
4 mushrooms
2 eggs
3 oz. grated cheese
2 tablespoons cream
salt and pepper

1 Line a flan ring with pastry.
2 Bake blind until crisp and golden in a hot oven (425–450°F.—Gas Mark 6–7).
3 Skin and chop the tomatoes; wash and chop mushrooms.*
4 Add remaining ingredients to beaten eggs.
5 Season well and pour into flan case.
6 Bake for 15–20 minutes in the centre of a moderate oven (375°F.—Gas Mark 4) until golden and set.

* Good cultivated mushrooms need not be peeled.

## Lattice flan

cooking time 40 minutes

**you will need for 4 servings:**

6 oz. cheese pastry (see page 53)
2 large onions
1 oz. margarine or fat
seasoning
1 tablespoon tomato ketchup
2 16-oz. cans baked beans in tomato sauce
2–3 oz. grated cheese
little beaten egg

1 Roll out pastry to $\frac{1}{8}$ inch thick and line an 8-inch flan ring. Cut trimmings into strips for the lattice top.
2 Fry finely chopped onion in margarine for 3 minutes; add seasoning and stir in the tomato ketchup.
3 Place the cooked onion mixture and the baked beans in tomato sauce in layers in the flan case, finishing with onions.
4 Sprinkle grated cheese over the top and weave the pastry strips across to form a lattice.
5 Brush the pastry with a little beaten egg and bake in the centre of a hot oven (450°F.—Gas Mark 7) for approximately 15 minutes, then lower heat to moderately hot (400°F.—Gas Mark 5) for a further 25 minutes.

## Leek flan

cooking time 30 minutes

**you will need for 4 servings:**

4 oz. self-raising flour (with plain flour 1 teaspoon baking powder)
salt and pepper
1 oz. butter or margarine
1 beaten egg
2 tablespoons milk

**For filling:**
1 lb. leeks
2 tablespoons thick cream
salt and pepper
4–6 oz. grated Lancashire cheese

1 Sieve flour with salt and pepper.
2 Rub fat into flour.
3 Stir in the egg and milk to make a soft dough.
4 Roll out and press dough into a greased 7-inch sandwich tin.
5 Chop leeks and boil until tender.
6 Chop leeks again and mix with cream and seasoning.
7 Spread over the dough and cover with grated cheese.
8 Bake at 450°F.—Gas Mark 7 for 25 minutes.

## Onion and mushroom flan

cooking time 45 minutes

**you will need for 4 servings:**

5 oz. short crust pastry (see page 55)
6 oz. sliced mushrooms
2 large thinly sliced onions
2 oz. margarine
2 eggs
2 tablespoons milk
seasoning
2 tablespoons grated cheese

1 Roll out pastry and line a sandwich or flan tin.
2 Bake 'blind' for about 10 minutes, so pastry is crisp but not brown.
3 Fry mushrooms and onion in margarine.
4 Put into the flan case.
5 Beat the eggs with the milk, add seasoning and cheese.
6 Pour over mushrooms and onions and cook for about 30 minutes in the centre of a moderate oven (375°F.—Gas Mark 4).

**Variations:**

### Onion and tomato flan

Substitute 8 oz. skinned tomatoes for mushrooms.

## Provencale flan

Use 1–2 cloves crushed garlic, 2 tomatoes, small red or green pepper, de-seeded and chopped, and 2 oz. cooked, diced carrots instead of mushrooms.

## Sweetcorn and egg flan

cooking time 25 minutes

**you will need for 4 servings:**

- 8 oz. short crust pastry (see page 55)
- ½ oz. margarine
- ½ oz. flour
- large can creamed sweet corn
- salt and pepper
- 4 eggs

1. Line an 8-inch plain flan ring with thin pastry; bake 'blind' in centre of moderately hot oven (400°F.—Gas Mark 5) until crip and golden brown.
2. Melt the margarine.
3. Blend in the flour and cook until mixture bubbles.
4. Add sweetcorn gradually, stirring constantly.
5. Bring to the boil and boil for 2–3 minutes, adding seasoning.
6. Meanwhile, poach the eggs (see page 30).
7. Place the poached eggs in the flan case and cover with the corn mixture.
8. Serve at once.

## Tomato and cheese flan

cooking time about 40 minutes

**you will need for 4 servings:**

- 1 lb. tomatoes
- 6 oz. short crust pastry (see page 55)
- 1 sliced onion
- 8 oz. breadcrumbs
- 3 oz. grated cheese
- seasoning
- 1 oz. butter

1. Cut all but one tomato into pieces.
2. Heat gently until pulped.
3. Line a pie dish with the pastry.
4. Fry onion lightly and mix with the tomatoes, half the breadcrumbs and half the cheese.
5. Season well.
6. Cover with the remainder of the cheese and breadcrumbs; dot with knobs of the butter.
7. Bake for approximately 20 minutes in the centre of a hot oven (450°F.—Gas Mark 7).
8. Reduce heat to moderate (375°F.—Gas Mark 4) for a further 20 minutes.
9. Garnish with remaining tomato finely sliced.

## Bean egg plate pie

cooking time approximately 45 minutes

**you will need for 4 servings:**

- 2 large onions, chopped
- 1 oz. butter or margarine
- 1 large can baked beans
- 1 tablespoon chopped parsley
- salt and pepper
- 12 oz. short crust pastry (see page 55)
- 4 eggs
- 1 egg or milk to glaze

1. Fry the onion in fat until soft.
2. Mix with beans, parsley and seasoning.
3. Roll out pastry and use half to line 8-inch pie plate.
4. Put in bean filling, break in eggs, cover with remaining pastry. Glaze pastry top.
5. Make an airhole in the pastry lid; bake in a moderately hot oven (400°F.—Gas Mark 5) for 40 minutes.
6. Serve hot or cold.

**Variation:**

Substitute a large can of spaghetti for the baked beans and follow as with the recipe above.

## Leek, egg and cheese pie

cooking time 30 minutes

**you will need for 4 servings:**

- 4 large cooked leeks
- 8 oz. short crust pastry (see page 55)
- 2 beaten eggs
- 2 oz. grated cheese
- seasoning
- little egg or milk for glazing

1. Drain the cooked leeks, then cut into 1-inch lengths.
2. Cover a pie plate with half the pastry, put leeks on top.
3. Add the cheese to eggs and season well.
4. Pour over the leeks.
5. Cover with second round of pastry.
6. Brush top with a little egg or milk and bake in the centre of a hot oven (450°F.—Gas Mark 7) for ½ hour. After 20 minutes, reduce heat to moderate (375°F.—Gas Mark 4). Serve hot or cold.

## Country pie

cooking time 45 minutes

**you will need for 4 servings:**

**For pastry:**
4 oz. plain flour
pinch salt
1½ oz. cooking fat
1½ oz. margarine or butter
1 tablespoon lemon juice
ice cold water
beaten egg or milk for glazing

**For filling:**
1 oz. cooking fat
1 large onion
4 mushrooms
seasoning
16 oz. can baked beans in tomato sauce

1 Sift flour and salt. Add the fats and cut into pieces.
2 Add lemon juice and sufficient iced water to make a stiff dough.
3 Turn on to a floured board and roll into an oblong strip, approximately 3 inches by 8 inches, keeping the edges straight.
4 Fold the pastry to one-third its present size by bringing the bottom third to the middle and folding over the top third.
5 Press the edges to enclose the air and turn the pastry to bring the fold on the left-hand side.
6 Repeat the rolling and folding process three times, allowing the pastry to stand in a cool place for 15 minutes after the second and fourth rollings.
7 Slice onion—quarter mushrooms.
8 While the pastry is standing after its fourth rolling, heat the fat and add the onions and mushrooms.
9 Add seasoning and fry for 10 minutes.
10 Add the baked beans, mix and put into a 1 pint pie dish.
11 Roll pastry to ¼ inch thick and 1¼ inches larger than the dish in all directions. Place over the pie.
12 Use the extra 1¼ inches to line the edge of the dish and to trim and flute for an attractive finish.
13 Decorate with pastry leaves and brush with beaten egg or milk.
14 Bake in the centre of a hot oven (450°F.—Gas Mark 7) for approximately 15 minutes, then lower heat to moderately hot (400°F.—Gas Mark 5) for about 30 minutes.

## Vegetable cheese pie

cooking time 25–30 minutes

**you will need for 4 servings:**

8 oz. cheese pastry (see page 53)
2 medium onions
2 tomatoes
1 oz. fat
4 oz. cooked peas
salt and pepper to taste
3 cooked chopped carrots
½ level teaspoon mixed herbs or thyme or 1 level dessertspoon chopped parsley
little beaten egg and/or milk for glazing

1 Chop onions and tomatoes coarsely, fry in fat, then mix all filling ingredients together.
2 Turn pastry on to lightly floured board, divide in half. Roll out one half and line an 8-inch well-greased ovenproof plate with it.
3 Moisten edges of pastry with water, pile filling in the centre; cover with remaining pastry, rolled out into a circle slightly larger than the plate. Press edges well together to seal, then knock up with the back of a knife.
4 Brush top with beaten eggs and/or milk and decorate with pastry leaves, rolled and cut from trimmings.
5 Bake in the centre of a hot oven (425–450°F.—Gas Mark 6–7) for 25–30 minutes.
6 Serve hot or cold with salad.

## Egg flaps

cooking time 20 minutes

**you will need for 4 servings:**

4 hard-boiled eggs

**For pastry:**
4 oz. plain flour
1 level teaspoon dry mustard
pinch salt
shake pepper
2 oz. butter
1½ oz. grated Cheddar cheese
1–2 tablespoons cold water
milk for glazing

1 Shell eggs.
2 Sift flour, mustard, salt and pepper.
3 Rub in butter, add cheese, then mix to a stiff paste with the water.
4 Turn on a lightly floured board, knead quickly until smooth.
5 Cut into 4 equal pieces.
6 Roll pieces out thinly, moisten edges with cold water, then wrap carefully around eggs, pressing edges of pastry together to seal.

7 Put on greased baking tray, placing each so that join is at the bottom.
8 Brush with milk and bake near top of hot oven (425–450°F.—Gas Mark 6–7). Cool, then serve.

## Cheese tarts

cooking time 15 minutes

**you will need for 4 servings:**

4 oz. short crust pastry (see page 55)
3 eggs
1 teaspoon grated onion
seasoning
2 teaspoons finely chopped parsley
3 tablespoons grated Parmesan cheese

1 Line patty tins with thin short crust pastry.
2 Beat eggs well and mix with onion, seasoning and parsley, and most of the cheese.
3 Put spoonfuls of the filling into the pastry.
4 Sprinkle with remaining cheese and bake in centre of a hot oven (450°F.—Gas Mark 7) for 15 minutes.

**Variations:**

### Mushroom tarts

2 oz. chopped cooked mushrooms instead of cheese.

### Tomato tarts

2 large skinned chopped tomatoes and 1 oz. breadcrumbs instead of cheese.

## Savoury raisin tarts

cooking time 15 minutes

**you will need for 4 servings:**

8 oz. shortcrust pastry (see page 55)
4 oz. grated Cheddar cheese
seasoning
2 beaten eggs
4 tablespoons white sauce (see page 63)
2 oz. seedless raisins

1 Line tart tins with pastry.
2 Mix the cheese, seasoning, eggs and sauce.
3 Put a few raisins in each tartlet case and a spoonful of the mixture on top.
4 Bake in the centre of a hot oven (450°F.—Gas Mark 7) for 15 minutes.
5 Serve hot or cold, with salad.

## Vol au vent cases from frozen puff pastry (Method 1)

cooking time 15–30 minutes depending on size

**you will need for 4 servings:**

1 packet frozen puff pastry
beaten egg for glazing

1 Roll out pastry, keeping the edges straight. You should need little, if any, flour on the board or pin.
2 Cut into rounds.
3 From half the rounds make rings by cutting out centres.
4 Place a ring on top of each round.
5 Seal edges and put on to DAMP baking trays.
6 Glaze with egg.
7 Bake in a very hot oven (475°F.—Gas Mark 8) until well risen, then reduce heat slightly to make sure pastry is cooked.

## Vol au vent cases from frozen puff pastry (Method 2)

cooking time 15–30 minutes depending on size

**you will need:**

1 packet frozen puff pastry
beaten egg for glazing

1 Roll out the puff pastry as in Method 1 (see above) and cut into rounds.
2 Put on to damp baking trays.
3 With a smaller cutter press half-way through pastry.
4 Glaze with egg.
5 Bake in a very hot oven (475°F.—Gas Mark 8) until well risen, then reduce heat slightly to make sure pastry is cooked.
6 Lift out the centre portion—this is quite easy to do with the point of a sharp knife, and return to the oven for a short time to dry out.

## Vol au vent cases (Method 3)

cooking time 15–30 minutes depending on size

It is possible to buy very good frozen puff pastry, but the recipe for home-made puff pastry is on page 54. Vegetarians can make this with vegetarian margarine, or part margarine and part vegetarian fat.

1 Make the puff pastry as the recipe.
2 After the complete number of rollings and foldings, put the pastry away for a while to set. Then roll to an oblong and use either Methods 1 or 2 as given in the instructions for the frozen puff pastry.

**To serve Vol au vents hot:**

1 Bake the pastry cases and keep warm.
2 Make the fillings.
3 Put together and serve at once.

**To serve Vol au vents cold:**

1 Allow both pastry and filling to become cold.
2 Put together and serve.

## *Fillings for vol au vent cases*

1 **Asparagus:** Use canned, fresh or frozen asparagus. If canned, open the can, pour off the liquid and measure. Use this to make a really thick sauce, i.e. 1 oz. butter or margarine, 1 oz flour, ¼ pint asparagus stock, or stock and milk. Add seasoning and just a little cream when the sauce has thickened. Put in the chopped tender base of the asparagus stalks, and add the tips when served in the pastry cases. With fresh or frozen asparagus, it must be cooked until tender and then treated as canned.
2 **Crab meat:** flaked and mixed with a little mayonnaise (see page 73) or sauce.
3 **Cucumber and egg:** mix diced cucumber and chopped hard-boiled eggs with a little thick mayonnaise. Season well.
4 **Eggs:** whether scrambled or hard-boiled, chopped and blended with mayonnaise, these can form the basis for a number of colourful fillings. Add grated carrot, cooked peas, grated cheese, or blend with mixed vegetables.
5 **Smoked haddock:** flaked and mixed with chopped hard-boiled egg and a little white sauce (see page 63). It can also be mixed with cheese sauce (see page 63).
6 **Mushrooms:** chopped, fried and stirred into a thick white sauce (see page 63).
7 **Tomatoes:** fried and used as a thick purée. They can be fried with mushrooms or chopped onions. If the mixture is a little slack because the tomatoes are rather juicy, then add some fine breadcrumbs.
8 **Prawns:** toss in lemon juice, season with black pepper and mix with a little mayonnaise (see page 73) or sauce. Garnish with whole prawns and a slice of lemon.
9 **Tuna:** drain and flake with a little mayonnaise (see page 73) or sauce.
10 **Anchovy:** drain and purée with a little mayonnaise (see page 73) or sauce. Garnish with strips of anchovy on the top and chopped parsley.

# Sauces

A sauce is not only a pleasant way of providing moisture and flavour to a dish, but since the basis of most sauces is fat and milk, it also adds extra food value.

An assortment of cooked vegetables served with a cheese or cheese and onion sauce makes a really satisfying main meal.

## Barbecue sauce

no cooking

**you will need for 4 servings:**

½ small onion
1 clove garlic
1 sprig parsley
¼ pint tomato ketchup
2 tablespoons wine vinegar
2 tablespoons corn oil
1 teaspoon Worcestershire sauce
ground pepper to taste

1 Mince onion, garlic and parsley and put into a large screw top jar with all the other ingredients.
2 Cover and shake vigorously until well blended.
3 Leave to stand for 24 hours, shaking occasionally.

## White sauce

cooking time 5–8 minutes

**you will need for 4 servings:**

1 oz. butter or margarine
1 oz. flour
½ pint milk for coating consistency
1 pint milk for thin sauce for soups
¼ pint milk for panada or binding consistency
seasoning

1 Heat the butter gently, remove from the heat and stir in the flour.
2 Return to the heat and cook gently for a few minutes so that the 'roux', as the butter and flour mixture is called, does not brown.
3 Again remove the pan from the heat and gradually blend in the cold milk.
4 Bring to the boil and cook, stirring with a wooden spoon, until smooth. Season well.
5 If any small lumps have formed, whisk sharply.

**Variations:**

### Anchovy sauce

Stir in chopped anchovies or 1 teaspoon anchovy essence.

### Cheese sauce

Stir in 3–6 oz. grated cheese when sauce has thickened, and add a little mustard.

### Caper sauce

Use ¼ pint milk and ¼ pint stock. Add 2 teaspoons capers and a little caper vinegar.

### Onion sauce

Boil 3 onions, chop or slice and add to sauce —use a little onion stock.

### Parsley sauce

Add 1–2 teaspoons chopped parsley and a squeeze lemon juice.

### Creamed tomato sauce

Whisk a thick tomato purée (which should be hot but not boiling) into hot white sauce. Do not boil.

### Horseradish sauce (hot)

Whisk about 1 dessertspoon vinegar and 2 tablespoons grated horseradish into white sauce. Add small amount of cream and pinch sugar.

### Mustard cream sauce

Blend ½–1 tablespoon dry mustard with the flour. Proceed as white sauce, stirring in little extra milk or cream.

### Béchamel sauce

Simmer pieces of very finely chopped onion, carrot and celery in milk. Strain and make as white sauce.

### Economical Hollandaise sauce

Make white sauce, remove from heat and whisk in 1 egg, 1 dessertspoon lemon juice or vinegar. Cook gently without boiling for a few minutes.

### Maître d'Hôtel sauce

As white sauce, but use half fish stock. Add 2 teaspoons chopped parsley and 3 tablespoons thick cream just before serving.

### Tartare sauce (hot)

Make white sauce, then whisk in 2 egg yolks, 1 tablespoon cream, 1 tablespoon chopped gherkins, 1 teaspoon chopped parsley and a squeeze lemon juice. Cook gently for a few minutes without boiling.

### Mushroom sauce

Cook 2 oz. chopped mushrooms in the milk, then use milk to make white sauce. Add cooked mushrooms and reheat.

## Cheese sauce with evaporated milk

cooking time 8 minutes

**you will need for 4 servings:**

small can evaporated milk
1 teaspoon made mustard
about 3 oz. grated cheese
seasoning

1 Put all the ingredients into a basin over hot water or into the top of a double saucepan.
2 Heat gently until the cheese has melted, stirring constantly.

## Cheese and onion sauce No. 1

cooking time 15 minutes

**you will need for 4 servings:**

1 finely chopped onion
1 oz. plain flour
⅜ pint milk
1 oz. butter
nutmeg
salt, pepper
4 oz. grated Cheddar cheese

1 Toss onion in heated butter for a few minutes, taking care it does not brown.
2 Stir in flour and cook for 2 minutes, then gradually add the milk.
3 Bring to the boil and cook until thickened, stirring constantly.
4 Stir in seasoning and cheese, and heat without boiling.

## Cheese and onion sauce No. 2

Following directions for onion sauce (see page 63) using ½ pint milk and, when the sauce has thickened, stir in 2–3 oz. grated cheese. Parmesan is the best for this sauce.

## Brown sauce

While the basis of a brown sauce is generally a meat stock, you can make a very good one by using water and yeast extract.

cooking time 10–12 minutes

**you will need for 4 servings:**

1½ oz. vegetarian fat or margarine (use dripping for a meat flavour)
1 oz. flour
seasoning
½ pint vegetable stock or water and yeast extract
little chopped onion and carrot (not essential but a distinct improvement)

1 If using the vegatables, chop finely and fry for a few minutes in the hot fat. Otherwise, just heat the fat. Stir in the flour and allow to become a golden brown, but be careful not to over-cook.
2 Gradually stir in the liquid, bring to the boil and cook until thickened.
3 Add seasoning to taste.
4 If using vegetables, the sauce can be strained before using.

You use the same variation in liquid to give the right consistency as in a white sauce (see page 63).

## Curry sauce

cooking time about 1 hour

**you will need for 4 servings:**

2 oz. butter or margarine
1 onion
1 apple
1 oz. flour
1 tablespoon curry powder or less if desired
1 teaspoon curry paste (optional)
salt, pepper
good pinch sugar
1 dessertspoon desiccated coconut
¾–1 pint stock (use meat stock for meat curries, fish stock or water for fish curries, water with a little yeast extract for vegetables or egg curries)
1 good tablespoon sultanas
1 good tablespoon chutney
squeeze lemon juice **or** few drops vinegar

1 Heat fat.
2 Fry finely chopped onion and apple until soft.
3 Stir in flour, curry powder and paste, and cook gently for several minutes. Add more curry powder to taste.
4 Gradually stir in the stock, bring to boil and cook until thickened.
5 Add other ingredients, tasting finally to make sure there is sufficient seasoning and sweetening.
6 Simmer the sauce for about 45 minutes at least, more if possible, then heat food to be curried in this.

## Cucumber sauce

no cooking

**you will need for 4 servings:**

1 large cucumber
salt and pepper
4 spring onions
1 jar yoghourt
1 tablespoon water
1 tablespoon wine vinegar

1 Peel and coarsely grate the cucumber, sprinkle with salt and leave for 10 minutes.
2 Chop onions finely and beat together with the yoghourt, water and pepper.
3 Drain water from cucumber, and add to the yoghourt mixture.
4 Stir in vinegar; add more seasoning if necessary.
5 Serve with cheese salad or cheese stuffed eggs.

## Tomato sauce No. 1

cooking time about 10 minutes

**you will need for 4 servings:**

1 oz. butter or margarine
1 small chopped onion
1 small grated apple
1 small tube or can tomato purée
2 level teaspoons cornflour
½ pint water
good pinch sugar
salt and pepper

1 Dice onion, carrot and crush clove of garlic, then add grated peeled apple.
2 Add the purée, the cornflour blended with the water, and seasoning.
3 Bring to the boil, and stir until smooth.
4 Simmer gently for about 10 minutes, taste and re-season, adding sugar if wished.

## Tomato sauce No. 2

cooking time about 30 minutes

**you will need:**

1 small diced onion
1 diced carrot
1–2 cloves garlic
1 oz. butter
5 large fresh or canned tomatoes
½ pint stock or liquid from can
½ oz. flour
1 bay leaf
salt and pepper
good pinch sugar

1 Dice onion, carrot and crush clove of garlic.
2 Heat butter and toss them in this. Do not brown.
3 Add tomatoes and simmer for a few minutes with canned tomatoes, rather longer with fresh ones. Take time doing this since it improves the flavour of the sauce.
4 Blend flour with stock, add to ingredients and simmer gently for about 30 minutes.
5 Stir from time to time.
6 Rub through a sieve or beat with a wooden spoon, add seasonings and sugar.
7 The bay leaf can be put in at the same time as the tomatoes but for a milder flavour add it with the stock.

## Piquante sauce

cooking time 10–15 minutes

**you will need for 4 servings:**

½ pint milk
bay leaf
2 teaspoons grated onion
2 oz. margarine or butter
3 or 4 large mushrooms
1 oz. flour
seasoning
1 teaspoon vinegar or lemon juice
Worcestershire sauce

1 Heat milk gently, together with the bay leaf and onion, and let it stand in a warm place for as long as possible.
2 Melt the margarine and fry the chopped mushrooms until just soft.
3 Blend in the flour with the milk; add to mushrooms and bring slowly to the boil, stirring all the time, until a smooth sauce; add seasoning.
4 Move pan from heat; whisk in the vinegar or lemon juice and the Worcestershire sauce.
5 Reheat without boiling.

Excellent with potato dishes or with pasta.

# Pancakes

Probably one of the most useful aspects about pancakes is that, apart from being extremely good to eat, they do use up any small quantities of food that is left.
The pancake batter given overleaf is the right pouring consistency. If made any thicker, you will have a too solid pancake.
Pancakes are always better if freshly cooked and eaten, but if you have to prepare beforehand, cook the pancakes at a convenient time, wrap and store in a cool place, then reheat for a few minutes.
On the other hand, pancakes can be cooked and kept hot over a pan of boiling water or on an uncovered dish in the oven.
If using a rather soft filling, keep the pancakes hot and the filling hot, putting the two together at the last minute.

## Pancake batter

cooking time 15 minutes

**you will need for 4 servings:**

4 oz. flour
pinch salt
1 egg
½ pint milk or milk and water
oil or fat for frying

1 Sieve flour into a bowl and add salt.
2 Make a well in the centre and stir in beaten egg and half the milk, mixed together. Beat lightly with wooden spoon for few minutes.
3 Add the remaining milk, and mix until batter is smooth.
4 Cover bowl and allow to stand in a cool place for 1 hour before using, if possible.
5 Melt fat in a thick frying pan and, when very hot, pour off excess fat.
6 Pour about 2 tablespoons of the batter or just enough to cover the bottom of the pan and cook over medium heat until set. Turn and cook other side until a golden brown.
7 Repeat until the rest of the batter is used.

## Savoury American pancakes

cooking time 15 minutes

**you will need for 6 servings:**

5 oz. plain flour
2 level teaspoons baking powder
1 level teaspoon castor sugar
½ level teaspoon salt
1 egg
½ pint milk
1 oz. melted butter or margarine

**For filling:**
creamed fish

1 Prepare filling.
2 Meanwhile heat girdle, skillet or frying pan gently.
3 Sieve flour, baking powder, sugar and salt into a mixing bowl.
4 Beat egg lightly, add the milk and melted fat, stir into the flour slowly, mixing only until batter is smooth.
5 When girdle is hot enough (a drop of water should splutter) grease lightly and pour batter from jug or spoon to form twelve 4-inch diameter pancakes.
6 When puffed and bubbly turn and brown other side.
7 Serve sandwiched and topped with filling.

**Variations:**

### American cheese pancakes

Make the pancakes as recipe above and sandwich together with a really thick cheese sauce (see page 63), to which can be added chopped cooked vegetables.

### Curry pancakes

Make a really thick curry sauce (see page 64) and add either cooked vegetables, chopped hard-boiled eggs, or flaked, cooked white fish to make the pancake filling.

## Spinach pancakes

cooking time 20 minutes

**you will need for 4 servings:**

1 lb. spinach
seasoning
1 oz. butter
4 oz. flour
1–2 beaten eggs
½ pint milk
fat for frying
½ pint white sauce (see page 63)
3 oz. grated cheese

1 Cook spinach with little seasoning—but little if any water.
2 Sieve the spinach and reheat with the butter.
3 Mix together flour, eggs, milk and seasoning.
4 Pour a little of this batter into hot fat in the pan and cook for several minutes until crisp and brown.
5 Turn or toss and cook other side.
6 Fill each pancake with some of the spinach. Keep hot on a dish over a pan of water.
7 When all the pancakes are cooked, add cheese to the white sauce and pour it over the top.

**Note:**

If preferred, all the pancakes may be kept flat and spread with spinach, piled on top of each other and then coated with sauce. To serve, cut into large slices as you would a cake.

**Variations:**

### Mixed vegetable pancakes

Fill with mixed vegetables—asparagus, fried mushrooms.

### Egg medley pancakes

Fry sliced tomatoes, mushrooms, with little chopped onion and/or chives and chopped parsley until a soft mixture. Add coarsely chopped hard-boiled eggs. Fill pancakes.

# Salads

One of the greatest advantages of a main meal salad is that it looks, or should look, really so full of colour that everyone will want to eat it immediately.

Salad greens are inclined to give a feeling of being very well fed for a time, but a salad is not a main dish unless it contains a fair percentage of protein foods.

In this chapter you will find a variety of salads —salads that are a meal in themselves, and those that are accompaniments.

No salad looks attractive unless the ingredients are crisp and fresh so, if you have to make it some time beforehand, cover with foil or one of the modern plastic coverings, and store in the coolest place possible.

Never put salads that are uncovered in a refrigerator, for the dry, cold atmosphere will spoil them. On the other hand, if you use an airtight container, a refrigerator is the ideal place.

## American salad

no cooking

**you will need for 4 servings:**

3 oz. celery
4 tomatoes
4–6 hard-boiled eggs
3 medium potatoes, cooked and diced
1 onion
vinaigrette sauce (see below)
lettuce

1 Chop celery, quarter tomatoes, slice eggs.
2 Combine potatoes, celery and onion slices, toss with a few tablespoons of vinaigrette sauce.
3 Arrange on lettuce, surrounded by tomato wedges, top with egg slices.
4 Serve additional vinaigrette sauce separately.

**To make the Vinaigrette sauce:**

3 tablespoons olive oil
¼ pint vinegar
salt, pepper, sugar, mustard to taste

Blend seasonings with oil, then add vinegar and stir vigorously until well mixed.

## Anchovy devilled eggs

no cooking

**you will need for 4 servings:**

6 hard-boiled eggs
2 teaspoons anchovy paste
1 teaspoon sugar
¼ pint mayonnaise (see page 73)
finely chopped parsley
watercress

1 Cut hard-boiled eggs in half lengthwise and remove yolks.
2 Mix egg yolks with anchovy paste, sugar and mayonnaise.
3 Fill egg whites with this mixture.
4 Sprinkle with parsley and serve on a bed of watercress.

**Variation:**

Replace the anchovy essence with 1 teaspoon curry powder, then continue as with the recipe above.

## Apple salad bowls

no cooking

**you will need:**

4 red dessert apples
lemon juice
peeled grapes
3 oz. diced shellfish
black olives
3 oz. diced Cheddar cheese
little top of milk
2 oz. chopped salted nuts

**To garnish:**
mint
parsley

1 Scoop out flesh of apples with grapefruit knife and brush inside of apples with lemon juice to preserve colour.
2 Fill hollowed out apples with peeled grapes, fish, black olives and apple flesh cut into neat dice.
3 Make small balls of grated cheese, mixed with a little top of milk and rolled in very finely chopped salted nuts.
4 Place individual 'baskets' on dish, decorate with sprigs of fresh mint and parsley, and serve with a bowl of well-flavoured mayonnaise (see page 73).

**Note:**

Cream cheese, flaked tuna fish or salmon could be used instead of shellfish.

## Autumn salad

no cooking

**you will need for 4 servings:**

1 white cabbage
1 finely chopped onion
2 oz. sultanas
2 grated raw carrots
4 oz. diced Cheddar cheese

1 Remove the outside leaves of the cabbage.
2 Shred finely and mix all the ingredients, finely chopped, together.

**Variation:**

Follow the recipe as above, but add 2 oz chopped roasted peanuts.

## Bean and cabbage salad

no cooking

**you will need for 4 servings:**

¼ teaspoon caraway seeds
2 tablespoons water
6–8 oz. finely shredded cabbage
medium can baked beans in tomato sauce
1 tablespoon grated onion or chopped chives
¼ pint sour cream
1 tablespoon vinegar
¼ teaspoon sugar
salt and pepper

1 Soak caraway seeds in water for 15 minutes and strain.
2 Chill cabbage and beans.
3 Mix and add onion or chives.
4 Combine sour cream, vinegar and sugar, pour over cabbage and beans.
5 Season to taste and toss lightly.
6 Sprinkle with caraway seeds.

## Broad bean salad

no cooking

**you will need for 4 servings:**

1 lettuce
1 lb. cooked young broad beans
½ small cucumber
3–4 tomatoes
8 oz. cooked green peas
3 cooked artichoke hearts
few spinach leaves
French dressing (see page 74)

1 Arrange the lettuce leaves on a large flat platter.
2 Place the broad beans in the centre.
3 Arrange the sliced artichoke hearts and remaining vegetables round the beans.
4 Before serving pour over the French dressing.

## Broad bean relish

no cooking

**you will need for 4 servings:**

1 small onion
3 sticks celery
2 hard-boiled eggs
2 medium cans broad beans
1 tablespoon mayonnaise (see page 73)
1–2 teaspoons made mustard
1 teaspoon curry powder
pinch pepper
relish

1 Chop onion, celery and eggs together.
2 Add drained beans and mix in mayonnaise, relish and other seasonings.
3 Serve cool.

## Fresh beet salad

no cooking

**you will need:**

1 large or 2 small beetroot
little olive oil
fresh lemon juice
1 lettuce
chopped parsley

1 Well scrub and peel raw beetroot and shred on fine shredder.
2 Add a little olive oil and fresh lemon juice and blend.
3 Pile on lettuce leaves; decorate with lettuce heart and fresh chopped parsley.

## *Cheese salads*

no cooking

Making a variety of cheese salads is done by using a different type of cheese and blending it with a large selection of ingredients. Cheese combines just as well with fruit as it does with chutney or pickles, so a cheese salad need never be monotonous.

### Blue cheese

This type of cheese, because of its 'bite', can be served with potato, watercress, lettuce, and chopped celery when in season, but it is also delicious if crumbled and piled on rings of apple. If the apple has a pretty skin, leave it unpeeled. Brush the apple with either a little French dressing or mayonnaise, which will prevent it discolouring.

## Cottage cheese

Because cottage cheese is low in calories, it is excellent in a slimming diet, apart from being delicious. All fruits, and in particular oranges, peaches, pineapple, as well as dates and nuts, blend extremely well with cottage cheese.

## Cream cheese

Because this has a delicate and rather rich flavour, although it varies a great deal according to type, you cannot only serve it with fruit and vegetables, but also with rather sharp ingredients such as gherkins or olives.

## Cheddar cheese

—and the great variety of other cheeses, such as Cheshire, Lancashire, Leicester or Double Gloucester, are all suitable for salads. Some people find cheese more digestible when grated. It looks very attractive if the grated cheese forms a pyramid in the centre of a gaily decorated dish, but the cheese can be diced, mixed with tossed potato, cucumber or beetroot (although this should only be added at the last minute as it tends to colour the cheese a great deal).

For a moulded salad you can put the ingredients into a basin press down gently and leave for a while.

## Processed cheese

If using slices of processed cheese, these look very attractive if rolled and arranged around Russian or potato salad. The small portions of processed cheese should be served on individual lettuce leaves and garnished with radishes or tomatoes.

## Cheese and anchovy salad

no cooking

**you will need for 4 servings:**

4 cooked potatoes
4 oz. grated cheese
1 small tin anchovies
seasoning
1 dessertspoon vinegar
lettuce
tomatoes
sliced cucumber

Slice the potatoes.

Put with the cheese, anchovies, including oil from the tin, a little seasoning—be sparing with the salt—and vinegar.

3 Toss together carefully.
4 Put in the centre of a ring of small lettuce leaves, sliced tomatoes and cucumber.

## Cheese-stuffed eggs

cooking time about 8 minutes

**you will need for 4 servings:**

4 eggs
salt and pepper
1 oz. butter
3 oz. grated Cheddar cheese
$\frac{1}{2}$ teaspoon made mustard
8 small rounds buttered brown bread

1 Hard boil the eggs, cool and cut in half lengthwise. Trim egg bases so they stand firmly.
2 Scoop out yolks and sieve.
3 Blend with salt, pepper and butter.
4 Mix in cheese and mustard; spoon filling into egg whites.
5 Place on bread rounds and serve with a crisp green salad.

## Cheese-stuffed peaches

no cooking

**you will need for 4 servings:**

lettuce
large can halved peaches
4 tablespoons cottage cheese
few raisins
few toasted almonds
2 tablespoons corn oil mayonnaise (see page 73)
1 tomato to garnish

1 Arrange the strained peaches on a bed of lettuce.
2 Mix the cottage cheese and mayonnaise together.
3 Fill peach halves with cheese mixture.
4 Stud with raisins and spiked almonds.
5 Garnish with tomato wedges.

## Curried celery sticks

no cooking

**you will need for 4 servings:**

3 oz. cream cheese
1 tablespoon chopped parsley
2 teaspoons mayonnaise (see page 73)
1 teaspoon grated onion
$\frac{1}{4}$ teaspoon curry powder
$\frac{1}{4}$ teaspoon salt
celery sticks

1 Blend all ingredients together for filling.
2 Stuff celery sticks with the mixture.
3 Cut into bite-size pieces.

**Note:**

Filling keeps well for days in refrigerator.

## Coleslaw salad

no cooking

**you will need for 4 servings:**

½ large or 1 small cabbage—it must be crisp and fresh
mayonnaise (see page 73)
seasoning

1 Toss the finely shredded cabbage in a generous amount of mayonnaise and season well.
2 That is the basis of a Coleslaw, but you can add other ingredients to give interest—finely chopped sweet apples and nuts, dried fruit, grated raw carrot or finely chopped spring onions.

**Variation:**

Follow the recipe as above, but add 2 grated carrots, 1 grated onion, 1 grated apple and a handful of chopped peanuts.

## Golden salad

no cooking

**you will need for 4 servings:**

lettuce
1 lb. cooked Jerusalem artichokes
3 hard-boiled eggs
little chopped parsley
little finely chopped spring onion or chives
1 teaspoon made mustard
1 tablespoon vinegar (preferably white)
2 tablespoons olive oil
seasoning

1 Line salad dish with lettuce.
2 Slice the artichokes thinly and arrange in the dish with chopped egg whites, parsley and chives.
3 Mash the yolks.
4 Gradually work the mustard, vinegar and oil into the yolks; season well and pour over the artichokes.

## Haricot bean salad

no cooking

**you will need for 4 servings:**

6 spring onions or 1 medium-sized onion, preferably pickled
either 1 medium-sized tin haricot beans or soak and cook 3 oz. beans (i.e. weight when dry)
2 gherkins
lettuce or endive
small piece celery
2 tomatoes (unless beans have been canned in tomato sauce)
seasoning
dessertspoon Worcestershire sauce

1 Chop the onions finely and mix with all the other ingredients.
2 Serve on a bed of lettuce or endive.

This makes a good accompaniment to cheese.

## Mad-rush salad

no cooking

**you will need for 4 servings:**

8 oz. grapes
2–3 oranges
2 bananas
1 eating apple
lettuce

1 Halve and pip the larger grapes, leave the others whole.
2 Peel 2 oranges and separate the segments.
3 Peel other orange and slice across thinly.
4 Peel and slice bananas.
5 Peel, core and thinly slice the apple.
6 Mix all together in a large fruit bowl.
7 Serve on bed of crisp lettuce, with Vinaigrette sauce (see page 67).

## Mushroom salad

no cooking

**you will need for 4 servings:**

8 oz. cooked sliced potatoes
4–6 oz. raw mushrooms
1 bunch watercress
4 sticks sliced celery
4 sliced hard-boiled eggs
mayonnaise (see page 73)

1 Mix all the ingredients together except 2 eggs.
2 Add the dressing, mix again and decorate with remaining sliced eggs.

**Variation:**

Follow the recipe as above, but add chopped spring onion.

## Oratava salad

no cooking

**you will need for 4 servings:**

3 shelled hard-boiled eggs
6 oz. Cheddar cheese
2 dessert apples
squeeze lemon juice
2 firm tomatoes
4 ripe bananas

1 Slice eggs, grate cheese finely.
2 Slice peeled, cored apples and sprinkle with lemon juice.
3 Peel and slice tomatoes.
4 Place apple slices on a flat serving dish and cover with banana slices.
5 Garnish alternately with tomato and egg slices.
6 Sprinkle all with a little of the grated cheese, pile the rest of the cheese in the centre.
7 Serve with mayonnaise (see page 73).

## Peach cheese salad

no cooking

**you will need for 4 servings:**

lettuce
8 oz. cream cheese
sliced olives
4 canned peach halves
1 oz. shelled walnuts
2 clusters grapes

1 Arrange lettuce on a plate and pile cheese on one half.
2 Garnish with olives.
3 Put peach halves on remaining lettuce and top with shelled walnuts.
4 Arrange grapes on either side.

**Variation:**

Substitute pineapple rings for canned peaches and follow the recipe as above.

## Pineapple mould salad

cooking time 5 minutes

**you will need for 4 servings:**

2 lemons
½ pint water
½ oz. gelatine
½ pint pineapple syrup from can
6 rings canned pineapple
lettuce
little cottage cheese
parsley to garnish

1 Simmer the lemon rind in the water for about 5 minutes; strain.
2 Dissolve gelatine in this.
3 Add lemon juice and syrup.
4 Stir well together and pour into individual moulds and allow to set.
5 Arrange pineapple rings on a bed of lettuce and fill the centre of each with cottage cheese.
6 Turn out a mould on to each pineapple ring, garnish with parsley.

## Potato salad (cold)

The best potato salads, even when served cold, are blended when hot, so unless you are using left-over potatoes, cook and mix the moment they are ready.

You can use a dressing of oil and vinegar as the Hot Potato Salad below, or you can blend with a little less oil and vinegar, and mayonnaise as well.

In addition, diced cucumber, celery, gherkins, capers and dessert apples add interest to potato salad, as well as onions and parsley.

## Potato salad (hot)

cooking time 25 minutes

**you will need for 4 servings:**

1 lb. potatoes
1 finely chopped onion
3 tablespoons oil
1 tablespoon vinegar
salt and pepper
parsley

1 Boil potatoes in their skins until just cooked.
2 Skin and cut into ¼-inch slices.
3 Cook the onion gently in the oil, add the vinegar, pepper and salt.
4 Pour over the potatoes and sprinkle with finely chopped parsley. Serve with cheese.

**Variation:**

Follow the recipe as above, but cook the onions in oil and coat the potatoes and onion with mayonnaise. Garnish with freshly chopped parsley.

## Hot potato cheese salad

cooking time 30 minutes

**you will need for 4 servings:**

1 lb. potatoes
1 finely chopped onion
3 tablespoons oil
1 tablespoon vinegar
salt and pepper
4–8 oz. diced cheese
parsley

1 Boil potatoes in their skins until just cooked. Skin and cut into ¼-inch slices.
2 Cook onion gently in the oil, add vinegar, pepper and salt.
3 Pour over the potatoes, add cheese.
4 Sprinkle with finely chopped parsley.

## Potter's salad

cooking time 20 minutes

**you will need for 4 servings:**

6 oz. flan pastry (see page 54)
2 pears
2 oz. cream cheese
4 oz. cooked carrots
4 tomatoes

1 Roll out the pastry and line a large flan tin.
2 Bake in a hot oven until crisp and brown (425–450°F.—Gas Mark 6–7).
3 When cold, place the pears, peeled, cored and cut in half, in the flan and top each half with the cream cheese.
4 Arrange the sliced tomato and carrots in the spaces between the halves.
5 Serve with a bowl of fresh lettuce.

## Rosy eggs

cooking time 10 minutes

**you will need for 4 servings:**

2 tablespoons brown sugar
¼ pint lemon juice
4 cloves
¼ teaspoon salt
5–6 small cooked beetroots
6 hard-boiled eggs

1 Mix together the sugar, lemon juice, cloves and salt.
2 Pour over the peeled and sliced beetroot and mix thoroughly.
3 Cook gently for about 10 minutes.
4 Add sliced eggs and serve cold.

## Russian salad

no cooking

**you will need for 4 servings:**

8 oz. cooked potato
8 oz. cooked carrots
8 oz. cooked peas
8 oz. runner or French beans
4 oz. cooked turnip
OR use cooked mixed frozen vegetables
2 tablespoons oil
1 tablespoon vinegar
seasoning
mayonnaise (see page 73)

1 Dice all vegetables except the cooked peas.
2 Put into a large bowl and pour over the oil and vinegar, then season well.
3 Leave for several hours, turning from time to time. Do this gently so the vegetables are not broken.
4 When ready to serve, pile on to a dish—or lettuce if desired—and form into a colourful pyramid.
5 Pour over just enough of the mayonnaise to coat lightly.

**Variation:**

Follow the recipe as above but add some flaked smoked fish, e.g. haddock, to the diced vegetables to make Russian Fish Salad.

## Seaman's salad

no cooking

**you will need for 4 servings:**

8 oz. cottage cheese
3 tablespoons top of milk
8 oz. shelled shrimps
4 oz. diced celery
1 level teaspoon celery salt
1 minced green pepper
1 tin pineapple
lettuce, or coleslaw (see page 70)

1 Sieve the cottage cheese and slowly blend in the milk.
2 Mix the remaining ingredients and serve on a bed of lettuce or coleslaw, decorated with the well-drained diced pineapple.

**Variation:**

Swop the shelled shrimps with 8 oz shelled prawns and follow the recipe as above.

## Tomato and cheese shape

cooking time 12 minutes

**you will need for 4 servings:**

1 oz. margarine
1 oz. flour
⅓ pint tomato purée
seasoning
2 heaped tablespoons breadcrumbs
2–3 oz. grated Cheddar cheese

1 Heat the margarine and carefully stir in the flour.
2 Cook for several minutes, then remove pan from the heat.
3 Gradually add the tomato purée and bring to the boil, stirring all the time.
4 Continue cooking until thickened.
5 Season well and add breadcrumbs while the sauce is hot, then the cheese.
6 Pour into a mould and allow to set.
7 Turn out and serve with salad.

## Stuffed tomato salad

no cooking

**you will need for 4 servings:**

- 2 medium-sized or 1 large tomato for each person
- 1 dessertspoon mayonnaise (see page 73)
- 1 dessertspoon chopped hard-boiled egg
- 2 tablespoons flaked fish
- seasoning
- lettuce

Slice tops off the tomatoes and carefully scoop out the centres.
Chop finely and mix all other ingredients.
Pile back into the tomatoes—if any filling is left, arrange in a ring around the tomatoes.
Serve with lettuce.

## Raw vegetable salad

no cooking

**you will need for 4 servings:**

- ½ small cabbage
- 2 carrots
- 1 small young turnip
- 1 medium-sized raw beetroot
- 2 tomatoes
- watercress
- oil and vinegar to taste
- seasoning

Shred the cabbage, and grate the other vegetables.
Slice the tomatoes.
Arrange in an attractive design on flat dish and add seasoning and dressing to taste.

Any other raw vegetables in season may be included—and, instead of cabbage, Brussels sprouts, spinach or cauliflower.

## Vinaigrette beans

no cooking

**you will need for 4 servings:**

- 1 large can broad beans
- 1 tablespoon chopped chives or tops of spring onions
- 2 tablespoons oil
- 2 tablespoons vinegar
- little chopped parsley
- seasoning
- sliced tomatoes

Open can of broad beans and drain liquid.
Blend with the chives, etc. and toss in all ingredients except the tomatoes.

3 Arrange thinly sliced tomatoes on a flat dish and top with the beans.
4 Serve as part of an hors d'oeuvre or a mixed salad.

## Classic mayonnaise

no cooking

**you will need for 4 servings:**

- 1 egg yolk
- good pinch salt, pepper and mustard
- ⅛–¼ pint olive oil
- 1 dessertspoon vinegar
- 1 dessertspoon warm water

1. Mix the beaten egg yolk and seasonings together.
2. Gradually beat in the oil, drop by drop, stirring all the time until the mixture is thick.
3. When it becomes creamy, stop adding oil as too much will curdle the mixture.
4. Beat in the vinegar gradually, then the warm water.
5. Use when fresh.

## Corn oil mayonnaise

no cooking

Recipe as Classic mayonnaise above, using ⅛–¼ pint corn oil instead of olive oil.

## Cream cheese salad dressing

no cooking

**you will need for 4 servings:**

- 4 oz. cream cheese
- pinch salt and pepper
- 1 teaspoon made mustard
- 2 tablespoons olive or corn oil
- 2 tablespoons milk or cream
- 2 tablespoons vinegar

1. Beat the cheese until very smooth.
2. Work in first the seasoning, then the oil.
3. Lastly, add the milk and vinegar.

**Variation:**

### Blue cheese dressing

Use blue cheese instead of cream cheese.

## Condensed milk mayonnaise

no cooking

**you will need for 4 servings:**

¼ pint sweetened milk
2 tablespoons oil
2 tablespoons vinegar or lemon juice
½ teaspoon salt
¼ teaspoon cayenne pepper
½ teaspoon dry mustard

1 Gradually mix all the ingredients together. Extra vinegar gives a more tart flavour.

## Egg mayonnaise

no cooking

**you will need for 4 servings:**

yolks of 2 hard-boiled eggs
¼ teaspoon dry mustard
pepper, salt
½ teaspoon sugar
⅛ pint cream or evaporated milk
1 tablespoon vinegar or lemon juice

1 Rub the egg yolks through a sieve or pound until very smooth, then add all the seasonings.
2 Gradually beat in the cream, then the vinegar, and continue beating until very smooth.

**Variations:**

## Curried mayonnaise

Add 2 teaspoons curry powder to the prepared mayonnaise.

## Garlic mayonnaise

Gently fold in 2-3 crushed cloves of garlic to the prepared mayonnaise.

## Fresh herb Mayonnaise

Add 1 tablespoon of your favourite chopped fresh herbs and 1 tablespoon of finely chopped spring onions to the prepared mayonnaise. This is a delicious dressing for potato salads.

## French dressing No. 1

no cooking

**you will need for 4 servings:**

6 tablespoons oil
1 level teaspoon sugar
seasoning
little made mustard
*3 tablespoons vinegar
little lemon juice

1 Blend oil into seasonings.
2 Gradually add vinegar and lemon juice.

*This dressing can be varied by different kinds of vinegar—red and white wine vinegar, tarragon vinegar, etc.

## French dressing No. 2

no cooking

**you will need for 4 servings:**

6 tablespoons corn oil
3 tablespoons vinegar
1 level tablespoon sugar
seasoning

1 Put all ingredients into a screw top jar and shake well.

## Spiced mayonnaise

no cooking

**you will need for 4 servings:**

yolks only of 2 hard-boiled eggs
¼ teaspoon dry mustard
pepper and salt
1 tablespoon mushroom sauce or ketchup
3 tablespoons olive oil
1 tablespoon Worcestershire sauce
2 tablespoons vinegar—preferably a mixture of malt and tarragon vinegars

1 Rub the egg yolks through a sieve or pound until smooth; then add all seasonings.
2 Gradually beat in first the oil, then the sauces, and lastly the vinegar.

# Dips

## Serving dips for light meals and parties

Dips are an unusual type of meal but they have certain advantages, whether for a family meal or for serving at a party.

With few exceptions, they need no cooking and therefore the preparation time is relatively small. Even when cooked, they can be made quickly. Rather small quantities for some recipes have been given because it is quite likely that if you are entertaining you will wish to have several types of Dip. If you are serving this as the main dish, then the number of people for whom it will suffice is given. In one or two cases it may seem rather small, but this is because the Dip is so rich that only a little is sufficient.

You will find that a party is not at all expensive either in ingredients or in preparation time, if some of these ideas are used.

### Avocado-Roquefort dip (1)

no cooking

**you will need for 4 servings:**

1 clove garlic, grated or chopped
2 oz. grated Roquefort cheese
2 tablespoons lemon juice
seasoning
2 very ripe avocados, peeled
¼ teaspoon salt
½ teaspoon chilli powder
1 teaspoon Worcestershire sauce

1 Combine all ingredients and beat well.
2 As this mixture tends to darken on standing, beat or stir it occasionally to keep it light.

### Avocado-Roquefort dip (2)

no cooking

**you will need for 4 servings:**

1 or 2 avocados, peeled
2 oz. grated Roquefort cheese
1 tablespoon lemon juice
olive oil
seasoning to taste

1 Press avocados through a sieve to make ½ pint purée.
2 Add cheese, lemon juice and enough olive oil to make a smooth consistency.
3 Add seasonings to taste; chill.

### Black bean soup dip

no cooking

**you will need for 4 servings:**

*1 can condensed black bean soup
6 oz. cream cheese
¾ teaspoon powdered thyme
1 teaspoon Worcestershire sauce
¼ teaspoon salt
¼ teaspoon powdered garlic

1 Beat together well to blend.
*When not available use condensed mushroom soup.

## Blue cheese dip

no cooking

**you will need for 4 servings:**

4 oz. blue cheese, crumbled
¼ pint chilli sauce
3 tablespoons salad dressing or mayonnaise (see page 73)
¼ teaspoon garlic salt
2 oz. chopped parsley
2 tablespoons minced onion

1 Combine all ingredients.
2 Blend well; serve well chilled.

## Cheese nut dip

no cooking

**you will need for 4 servings:**

3 oz. cottage cheese
3 oz. cream cheese
¼ pint sour cream
dash Tabasco sauce
pinch garlic powder
pinch black pepper
¼ teaspoon salt
3 oz. chopped nuts

1 Blend all the ingredients together; chill thoroughly.
2 Serve with chips or corn.

## Chilli con quesco

cooking time 15 minutes

**you will need for 3 servings:**

1 onion
*2 green chillis, peeled
2 tablespoons bacon fat
*¼ pint red chilli purée
6 oz. processed cheese
salt, pepper and garlic salt

1 Fry onion and chillis in fat until light brown.
2 Add chilli purée and cheese cut into small cubes.
3 Reduce heat and simmer, stirring constantly, until all cheese is thoroughly melted, but do not allow to boil.
4 Season to taste.
5 Serve piping hot.
*This makes an unbelievably hot dip—so warn people and serve with plenty of crisp bread. For a milder dip, use 1 small green capsicum—and 1 large red capsicum. Remove pips and core and chop finely.

## Clam dip

no cooking

**you will need:**

1 teaspoon lemon juice
1 teaspoon Worcestershire sauce
medium can minced clams, drained
6 oz. cream cheese

1 Add lemon juice and Worcestershire sauce to clams.
2 Mix with the cream cheese.
3 Chill and serve.

## Fontina dip

cooking time 10–12 minutes

**you will need for 4 servings:**

1 tablespoon butter
3 tablespoons flour
scant 1 pint milk
1 lb. Emmental or similar cheese
pinch salt
pepper
nutmeg
French bread

1 Melt butter over hot water.
2 Add flour and blend well.
3 Stir in milk, a little at a time.
4 Bring to a boil and add cheese, stirring constantly with a fork, until melted.
5 Add seasoning to taste.
6 Serve very hot, with cubes of French bread, or small cheese biscuits.

### Variation:

If you like, add ¾ pint of dry cider instead of the milk and continue as with the recipe above.

## Garlic cheese dip

no cooking

**you will need for 8 servings:**

8 oz. cottage cheese
⅛ pint milk
2 cloves garlic, crushed
salt

1 Combine cheese, milk and garlic.
2 Force through a fine sieve or whip in an electric blender.
3 Add a generous amount of salt and, if necessary, a little more milk to make a dip soft enough to pick up on potato chips.

## Guacamole dip

no cooking

**you will need for 4 servings:**

3 tablespoons finely chopped onion
1 tomato, peeled and chopped
2 avocados, peeled and mashed
1 teaspoon salt
2 teaspoons chilli powder
1 tablespoon lemon juice

1 Combine the onion, tomato and avocados, mash until smooth.
2 Add salt, chilli powder and lemon juice.
3 Mix well.

**Variation:**

Follow the recipe as above, but omit the chilli powder and add 1 deseeded and finely chopped fresh green chilli.

## Dip and Dunk Tray

This is a real party piece that takes minutes to get ready. A central bowl of mayonnaise (see page 73) with mustard and chopped nuts added. Surround this with separate dishes of small biscuits, potato chips and celery curls. Other little dunks can be made of cheese, gherkins, olives, tiny croquettes of tuna fish, bound with white sauce (see page 63) and deep fried. Cocktail sticks are essential for this kind of dunk.

## Parmesan garlic dip

no cooking

**you will need for 4 servings:**

¼ pint evaporated milk
6 oz. cream cheese, softened
2 teaspoons grated onion, or ½ teaspoon onion powder
¼ teaspoon garlic powder
1 teaspoon Worcestershire sauce
2 oz. grated Parmesan cheese

1 Gradually add milk to cheese, blending well.
2 Add remaining ingredients; mix thoroughly.
3 If dip is too thick, add more milk until mixture is the desired consistency.

## Onion soup dip

no cooking

**you will need for 4 servings:**

1 packet onion soup mix
1 pint sour cream
Tabasco sauce

1 Mix together soup mix and sour cream until well blended.
2 Add a touch of Tabasco and serve as a dip.
3 If dip becomes too thick while standing, thin with more sour cream.

## New Roquefort dip

no cooking

**you will need for 4 servings:**

6 oz. cream cheese
2 oz. Roquefort cheese
1 tablespoon thick cream
¼ tablespoon onion juice
1 tablespoon sherry

1 Blend all ingredients, using more Roquefort if needed to make a creamy consistency.
2 Let stand for a few hours before serving.

## Pimento cream cheese dip

no cooking

**you will need for 4 servings:**

6 oz. cheese, preferably cream cheese
1 pimento, minced
3 oz. ripe olives, chopped
1½ oz. walnuts, chopped
Tabasco sauce to taste
cream

1 Combine all ingredients and blend, using enough cream to make mixture a good dipping consistency.
2 Serve with corn or potato chips.

## Vegetable dunking bowl

no cooking

**you will need for 5–6 servings:**

1 lb. cottage cheese
3 oz. finely cut spring onions
1½ oz. grated raw carrot
⅛ pint cream
4 radishes, sliced
1½ oz. chopped green pepper
salt to taste
sprigs of 1 cauliflower and carrot strips

1 Blend all ingredients except cauliflower and carrot together in food blender.
2 Serve in a bowl with crisp carrot strips and cauliflower sprigs for dunking.

## Roquefort dip

no cooking

**you will need for 3 servings:**

6 oz. cream cheese
Roquefort cheese to taste
1 tablespoon thick cream
¼ teaspoon onion juice
1 tablespoon sherry

1 Blend all ingredients using enough Roquefort to make creamy consistency.
2 Let stand for a few hours, before serving with chips, corn or cream crackers.

## Cottage cheese and pineapple dip

no cooking

**you will need for 4 servings:**

12 oz. cottage cheese
1 small can pineapple pieces
2 oz. finely chopped walnuts
seasoning
lettuce

**To garnish:**
few chopped walnuts
1 teaspoon chopped chives

1 Blend cottage cheese with chopped drained pineapple pieces, and walnut.
2 Season well and arrange in bed of lettuce in shallow bowl.
3 Garnish with nuts and chives.
4 Serve with potato crisps or cheese biscuits.

## Leek cream dip

no cooking

**you will need for 4 servings:**

packet leek soup powder
2 oz. grated cheese
seasoning
¼ pint yoghourt, sour cream or fresh cream and little lemon juice

**To garnish:**
1 oz. coarsely grated cheese
1 oz. chopped walnuts
watercress

1 Blend leek soup powder with other ingredients.
2 Put into shallow bowl and top with ring of cheese and walnuts.
3 Garnish with watercress sprigs.

## Tomato and cream cheese dip

no cooking

**you will need for 4 servings:**

4 large tomatoes
12 oz. cream cheese
salt, pepper
cayenne pepper
little chopped chives or spring onion

**To garnish:**
onion rings

1 Skin tomatoes, rub through sieve.
2 Blend with other ingredients; put into shallow bowl.
3 Top with onion rings.
4 Serve with fingers of crispbread.

## Sour cream and olive dunk

no cooking

**you will need for 4 servings:**

1 pint thick sour cream
4½ oz. finely chopped ripe olives
1 tablespoon grated onion
salt and pepper to taste

1 Combine all ingredients and use as a dunk for raw vegetables.

# Savoury Spreads—Sandwich Fillings

Many people feel that sandwich fillings without meat are not particularly sustaining or interesting, but this, of course, is wrong. There is a wide selection of sandwich fillings which are just as nutritious. This chapter includes some unusual ones, and others that are quickly and easily prepared.

## Cheese and red caviar

no cooking

**you will need for 4 servings:**

- 4 oz. cream cheese
- 2 tablespoons cream
- 1 teaspoon onion juice
- 1 teaspoon lemon juice
- 2 tablespoons red caviar

1. Soften cream cheese with cream and onion juice.
2. Add lemon juice and mix in the caviar very carefully to avoid breaking it.
3. Serve with dark rye bread.

**Variation:**

Substitute 2 tablespoons of lump fish roe for the caviar and continue as in the recipe above.

## Cheese and cods' roe

no cooking

Use the same recipe as above, but add approximately 4 oz. cooked cods' roe instead of caviar.

## Curried olive spread

no cooking

**you will need for 4 servings:**

- 3 oz. cream cheese
- 2 tablespoons milk
- $\frac{1}{8}$ teaspoon curry powder
- $\frac{1}{4}$ teaspoon onion powder
- 2 oz. chopped ripe olives
- dash pepper and paprika

1. Mix cream cheese and milk until smooth and of spreading consistency.
2. Add remaining ingredients and blend.
3. Serve as a spread or in sandwiches.

## Egg and Swiss cheese spread

no cooking

**you will need for 4 servings:**

- 6 hard-boiled egg yolks, sieved
- mayonnaise to bind (see page 73)
- salt and pepper
- 4 oz. grated Gruyère or Emmental cheese
- 1 teaspoon prepared mustard

1. Blend, using enough mayonnaise to bind ingredients to a smooth paste of spreading consistency.

**Variations:**

Other cheese can be used in place of the Swiss cheese given above.

In particular, a Blue or cream cheese are excellent.

If using cream cheese, for a really good bite', add a little extra mustard.

## Liptauer spread

no cooking

**you will need for 4 servings:**

| | |
|---|---|
| 6 oz. cream cheese | 1 teaspoon capers |
| 1 can anchovies | 1 teaspoon caraway seeds |
| 1 tablespoon butter or margarine | 1 teaspoon paprika |
| | 1 teaspoon chopped onion |

1 Ingredients must be at room temperature.
2 Combine all ingredients; mix thoroughly.

## Lobster and cucumber spread

cooking time 5 minutes

**you will need for 4 servings:**

| | |
|---|---|
| 4 oz. lobster meat, chopped fine | 1 small cucumber, chopped fine |
| melted butter | salt |
| mayonnaise (see page 73) | paprika |

1 Sauté lobster in butter.
2 Cool; add cucumber.
3 Season and use enough mayonnaise to make spreading consistency.

**Variations:**
Crab meat, chopped shrimps or prawns, can be used instead of the lobster meat. Tossing in butter first ensures a moist texture.

## Roquefort cheese spread

no cooking

**you will need for 4 servings:**

| | |
|---|---|
| 8 oz. Roquefort cheese | 12 oz. cream cheese |
| | port wine |

1 Blend cheeses and enough port wine to form a paste.
2 Chill thoroughly.

## Chive balls

no cooking

**you will need for 4 servings:**

| | |
|---|---|
| 6 oz. cream cheese | 1 teaspoon French mustard |
| 3 oz. chopped chives or chopped spring onions | ½ teaspoon salt |
| | ½ teaspoon pepper |

1 Cream well and shape into balls.
2 Serve on cocktail sticks.
3 Can also be used as dip or spread, adjusting consistency by adding sufficient cream or top of the milk.

**Variation:**

Substitute 2 tablespoons freshly chopped parsley for the chives to make parsley balls.

# Sandwich fillings

## Anchovy and egg

Chop canned anchovies finely and mix with hard-boiled egg or egg scrambled without salt. Serve on crisp lettuce.

## Beetroot

Grate equal quantities of cooked beetroot and cheese. Blend with a very little mayonnaise (see page 73) and shredded lettuce.

## Cucumber and egg

Finely grate cucumber and mix with chopped hard-boiled egg, watercress and mayonnaise (see page 73).

## Chutney and cheese

Mix grated cheese, chutney and a little raw grated carrot.

## Date and cheese

Blend chopped dates and a little chopped canned pineapple if wished, with cream cheese and shredded lettuce.

## Egg and chives

Mix finely chopped chives with scrambled egg and a little diced gherkin or cucumber.

## Fish

White fish, as well as canned or shellfish, can be mixed with mayonnaise and a very small amount of grated cucumber or chopped gherkin. With the oil fish, such as sardines, a tiny amount of grated apple gives a pleasant 'bite'.

## Kippered spread

There are two ways of using kippers as a sandwich filling.

The first is to cook them lightly, then flake the fish and blend with margarine or butter and chopped parsley; serve on lettuce.

Or use the kippers uncooked; bone fillets and leave a while, covered with a small amount of oil, vinegar, pepper. Drain well and put on crisp lettuce. These have a remarkable likeness to smoked salmon as a sandwich filling.

## Mushroom

Chop and fry mushrooms; drain and mix with chopped hard-boiled egg or grated cheese and a little mayonnaise (see page 73) or with grated raw carrot.

## Orange

Sliced oranges are so juicy, they are not good in closed sandwiches, but add colour and flavour to the open type. Mix small portions with grated or processed cheese or with a mixed salad filling.

## Tomato spread

Sliced tomatoes make bread damp, so it is better to skin and chop them. Then blend with the margarine or butter used in spreading. Only if the sandwiches are to be served soon after making, are sliced tomatoes by themselves or mixed with other ingredients recommended.

To add to your basic Tomato Spread, however, try the following:—

(a) Grated cheese and carrot.

(b) Grated cheese and chopped gherkins or cucumber.

(c) Flaked fish.

(d) Chopped hard-boiled eggs.

(e) Finely chopped red or green pepper and chopped watercress.

## Cheese and sweetcorn

Blend equal quantities of cream cheese and cooked or well drained canned sweetcorn together. Add a little chopped chives and grated Parmesan cheese for extra 'bite'.

## Cheese and walnut

Blend 2 oz chopped walnuts into 4 oz cream cheese and add some chopped chives

## Cheese and sesame

Mix 2 tablespoons sesame seeds into 4 oz cream cheese and add a little lemon juice.

## Egg and red pepper

Mix narrow strips raw red pepper (capsicum) with lightly scrambled eggs.

## Sardine and gherkin

Mash sardines, season well and mix with finely chopped pickled gherkins and chopped parsley. If using sardines in tomato sauce add few drops of lemon juice.

## Vegetable

It is possible to make sustaining salad fillings by mixing either very well drained, cooked vegetables (carrots, peas or beans), with a little mayonnaise, grated cheese and shredded lettuce; or use a variety of grated raw vegetables. Most vegetables are delicious grated raw and give an enjoyable bite and crispness to a sandwich. Mix two or three of the following: beetroot, carrots, endive, chicory or celery, gherkins or cucumber, red and green peppers, onions, swede, turnip. Moisten with a very little mayonnaise and top with slices of cheese or hard-boiled egg.

# Index